"Sheard's *An Introduction to Christian Belief* covers many of the topics that are important in any Catholic introductory course in a style that is readable and engaging. His positions are intelligent and balanced. This book should work well in conjunction with biblical and other primary texts."

Dennis M. Doyle
Author, *The Church Emerging from Vatican II*
University of Dayton, Ohio

"Robert B. Sheard has produced a suitable text, neither too advanced nor too simplistic, to teach undergraduate students the basics of Christian faith: namely, the nature and dynamics of Revelation and the person of Jesus.

"Sheard integrates the best insights of the old and new Christian theological schools in a clear, conversational style, succeeding because of his deep sense of the historical development and of the profoundly human character of the content of Christian belief.

"This well-organized book will certainly stimulate college students or adult parishioners to new and exciting paths of reflection regarding their faith."

Dr. Jacques Goulet
Mount Saint Vincent University
Former President of the Canadian Society for
the Study of Religion

"This is an exciting book for anyone who is searching for an understanding of his or her faith. It begins where people are in their everyday lives, poses important questions, and leads the seeker to a deeper level of understanding. Robert Sheard knows how to present the basics of our faith in an appealing manner. An excellent introduction to Christianity for students at the college level!"

Martin Moser
Dean of Theology
Newman Theological College
Edmonton, Canada

An Introduction to
Christian
Belief

A Contemporary
Look at the
Basics of Faith

ROBERT B. SHEARD

TWENTY-THIRD PUBLICATIONS
Mystic, CT 06355

Twenty-Third Publications
185 Willow Street
P.O. Box 180
Mystic, CT 06355
(860) 536-2611
800-321-0411

ISBN 0-89622-707-3
Library of Congress Catalog Card Number 96-60777
Printed in the U.S.A.

PREFACE

This book arises out of my experience of teaching undergraduate courses in theology at a Catholic college. In my search for a suitable basic text, no one introductory textbook seemed to cover what was needed if students were to acquire a proper understanding of the basic elements of theological reflection and of what is taking place today in the Christian Tradition. The textbooks I examined and used in class were either too advanced, presupposing too much prior theological background and thus unintelligible, or too simplistic, so that students were left with but a superficial, and possibly misleading, understanding. My hope is that *An Introduction to Christian Belief: A Contemporary Look at the Basics of Faith* will satisfy the need for a sound, intelligible introduction to Christian theology, one that charts a middle path between those texts that are too advanced and those that are too superficial.

In order to encourage and facititate reflection on the part of the student I have added Questions for Reflection and Discussion, as well as Suggested Readings for those who wish to go outside this text and read other presentations of the topics and issues the text discusses.

These pages will inevitably reflect the Catholic context and background from which I do my theological work. Most of the examples I use come from that tradition as will the emphasis I give to certain questions. Yet there is among theologians today a great amount of interdenominational kinship. In fact, with some of these topics—

Scripture, for example—mainstream Catholic, Anglican, and Protestant theologians will be in basic agreement and be opposed by people in their own tradition. Although I write from a Catholic context, Christians of other denominations should be able to share my concerns and enter into a useful dialogue with what I say.

This book, intended to be an introduction to the exciting field of Christian theology, will not answer all questions. If it stimulates the reader to a new and exciting path of reflection, it will have served its purpose.

Important changes are taking place in Christian thinking in our day. I hope the reader will feel drawn into the theological enterprise so that his or her search for and commitment to truth will continue and, indeed, become more and more a part of life.

Contents

An Introduction to Christian Belief

PART ONE

FUNDAMENTAL BELIEFS

INTRODUCTION

In the sixteenth century, the astronomer Nicolaus Copernicus made the astounding claim that planet Earth was not immovably at the center of the universe but that it moved, and it moved around the sun! This claim was more than a simple statement of astronomical fact. It was a claim that necessitated a radically new understanding of reality for the people of Copernicus's day. It involved the nature of religious truth and the very place of humans in the universe. Humans were, people thought, exalted beings with a dignity that was reflected even in the structure of the cosmos, since they had been placed by God on Earth at the very center of all things. What is more, the authority of the Bible, God's Word to humankind, supported this view, for the Bible talked about the sun moving around Earth. Hadn't Joshua command-ed the sun to stay still in its course around Earth so that he could have enough daylight to complete his defeat of the Amorite kings who fought against him (Joshua 10:1–15)? Copernicus's view profoundly challenged all of this. And it was not until some hundred years later that people came to accept this new worldview.

In contemporary Christian thinking, something of a Copernican revolution is taking place. Christians are challenging and replacing many of their traditional attitudes and ways of understanding reality and their faith. Just as people had to rethink their religious and social ideas as a result of the Copernican worldview, so today Christians are having to rethink and express in new ways what they believe about God, nature, and human existence in light of changes in their world-view. This should not be surprising, since in fact Christians have always done this, often unconsciously, and they will do the same for generations to come.

What is this new worldview? How does it affect the way Christians talk about and think about their faith? These are questions we will address throughout the course of this book as we explore fundamental changes that are taking place in Christianity today. These changes are so fundamental that the image of a Copernican revolution can legitimately be used as a way of describing them.

Our worldview is basically the way we understand reality in all of its aspects as a result of our interaction with the reality that surrounds us. It includes such things as the way we understand how the universe operates, how we understand the place and meaning of human exis-tence, what we regard as real and unreal, how we arrive at an under-standing of truth, what we judge as valuable, and so on. Although there are many differences in the way we experience and understand reality that have an impact on how we experience and understand the Christian faith today, there are two major aspects of our worldview that are crucially important. They are: 1) the recognition of the histori-cal relativity of human existence and thought; and 2) the recognition of the profoundly human character of all aspects of Christianity.

HISTORICAL-CULTURAL CONTEXT

One of the most important features of the contemporary worldview is the realization that human existence and human thought are histori-cally conditioned. This means that how we understand and talk about reality is affected by our historical and cultural situation, that is, the particular place we are at a particular time in history. We are limited beings who operate out of a limited context; we inherit and are brought up in a culture that has a past and so has developed particu-lar ways of thinking and acting. Our culture continues to develop dif-ferent ways of thinking and acting as we interact with our surround-ings and as we develop different ways of looking at things and make use of different technologies. There is, then, a profoundly contextual nature to our thinking and acting as these take place within a particu-lar culture and society and have meaning within them. If this context changes, our understanding and the meaning we assign to events change as well.

An example from language will illustrate this limited, contextual nature of human thought and existence. The words we use have meaning within a particular context and historical situation. The same word in a different time and in a different context can have quite a different meaning. Take, for example, the Christmas carol "Deck the Halls." One of the verses goes "Don we now our *gay* apparel." In the carol, the word "gay" has nothing to do with special homosexual clothing. For most people today, however, the word "gay" has taken on a homosexual connotation as its primary meaning. For us today, a "gay" man is not so much a happy, jolly man, which was the earlier meaning of the word, as he is a homosexual man. That was not so when that Christmas carol was written. The point is that our words have meaning in a particular time and place and their meanings can change when the context changes. A word does not "hang loose," as it were, unrelated to the total context in which it is used.

It is like this with all human thought and expression, even with religious affirmations. What Christian Tradition says will reflect when and where it is said. And like the example of the word "gay," changes in the historical context might very well necessitate a change in the way Christians think and talk concerning their convictions about reality. For example, when the concept of a world evolving over a long period of time supplants the worldview of ancient times, which held an essentially stable and static universe, it means that what Christians say about reality that reflects the old worldview must change if Christians are to present a credible, intelligible understanding of reality. Thus, they can no longer hold to the view that the universe took only six days to develop, as the Bible expresses it. To take another example, what we have learned about human development from evolution makes the image of a perfect pair of humans, Adam and Eve, existing at the beginning of human history free from suffering and death, incredible to our ears.

Part One of *An Introduction to Christian Belief*, especially the chapters on Scripture and Tradition, will expand on this more, and those in Part Two will look at some central Christian teachings that are being reformulated today simply because their past formulations were expressed in ways that reflect a very different understanding of reality than the one we now have.

Does this mean that everything is relative, that there is no abiding, firm foundation to our religious faith? This question will be addressed later, but it can be said here that the firm foundation we seek is God alone, and that the things we think and say about God, while they do lead us to the reality of God in some way, do so in a historically conditioned way, and therefore in a relative way. Of course, this needs to be developed further; not everything we say about God will necessarily do this. The Catholic Tradition, for example, holds that the Bible and the doctrinal tradition of the church are privileged places that mediate the truth about God, ourselves, and our world. But even these are historically conditioned formulations of truth. Their truth value lies in their power to put us in touch with the Divine. Yet they do so *truly*. This has to be emphasized. There is no foundationless relativity.

THE HUMAN DIMENSION

All these considerations depend on yet another dimension of the new way of understanding things that constitutes Christian reflection today. This is the recognition of the profoundly human character of Christian Tradition. In the past, there was a tendency to stress the divine side of things; God was so much behind everything connected to Christianity that humans did very little except to receive what God gave. For example, God inspired the authors of the Bible to write, the result being God's Word; God revealed "truths" to us that were unchanging and not affected by historical contexts; God willed that the church be set up in a particular way with a particular structure. While the human element was not entirely neglected, the stress was on divine activity; humans were largely passive receivers of God's action and God's absolute truths.

There has been, however, a shift toward the human in current Christian thinking. That is, there has emerged the awareness that humans have been and are very heavily involved in the way Christianity has taken shape. Humans are more than passive receivers of divine activity; rather, they actively condition and shape what Christian Tradition says and does.

These two features of our contemporary worldview—the historical and cultural nature of human thought and activity, and the active shaping of Christian Tradition by human beings—are the two most important features affecting Christian reflection and practice today. They account for the fact that our past formulations and practices may seem strange or inadequate and need to be reformulated if they are to make sense. And when Christians decades and centuries from now live in a different cultural environment with its different understanding of reality, they will have to reformulate Christian beliefs if they are to make sense to the people at that time. This is the fundamental conviction that grounds much of what is said in the pages that follow.

THEOLOGY

This is a book that *does* Christian theology. Because of this, it is useful to consider at the start what theology means and what it tries to do. An old and excellent definition of theology is "faith seeking understanding."[1] A more elaborate definition is this: "Theology may be defined as that study which, through participation in and reflection upon a religious faith, seeks to express the content of that faith in the clearest and most coherent language available."[2]

The various components of this definition are worth considering. Theology is a "study," a word that implies an intellectual discipline; it demands the use of one's mind, in other words. This cannot be emphasized enough since there are many who feel reluctant to reason about their faith, thinking that to question their religious faith is to question God in some way. And who ought to do that? Theology, as a reflective discipline, is based on the view that God has given human beings minds to use and calls upon them to use their minds to the utmost in learning about God and understanding their religious faith. Theologians insist that human beings do not have to exclude their rational, thinking powers when it comes to their faith commitments. Rather, they are called upon to exercise their reasoning relentlessly as they seek to understand, convinced that reason and faith are entirely compatible.

Theology involves "participation" in a religious faith. Theologians are believers, members of a religious community. Thus they are committed persons, sharing a particular faith vision; they do their thinking out of a basic commitment to a faith. In this, they differ from those who reflect upon religion and religious events from the perspective of a Religious Studies department in a college. These people claim no faith commitment in doing their work; they claim to be neutral observers, detached, free from biases that may distort their reflection and study. The question that theologians must address in all of this is whether their commitment to a particular religious faith gets in the way of really asking serious questions and critiquing that faith. Does the commitment to a particular faith bias a person so much that it is impossible to carry out honest reflective work and sincerely search for the truth? The answer is that such commitment can indeed hinder the sincere search for truth, but it need not. In fact, the best theologians do critique their faith and its expressions; they do commit themselves to search for the truth no matter where it leads them. Commitment to a religious vision and rigorous searching for the truth are not necessarily incompatible. This should become clear throughout the course of this book.

Theology involves a "religious" faith. Most, if not all, persons want to commit themselves to some central, overriding purpose or cause, or even to another person who has high ideals. A religious faith involves a commitment to some transcendent reality, that is, to a reality beyond the things or powers or persons we "normally" encounter in the universe. When it comes to religious faith, there is a commitment to "something more," something beyond ourselves and our world.

Moreover, theologians are concerned with the content of their religious faith. All religions make statements about reality. For example, Christianity says that the world was created by God, that humans are saved by Jesus, that God is good, and so forth. Hinduism, Islam, Judaism, too, all make certain claims about reality. What each of these religions teaches makes up the content of its faith. A primary task of the theologian and of theology is to make the content of religious faith understandable to contemporary human beings. This means, among other things, that what theologians say must be compatible with other well-founded knowledge we have. The understanding of reality that reason can attain through philosophy and the empirical sciences plays a role in the theological enterprise. Theology should not be talking about a world that is alien to the one that people live in and experience.

SCOPE OF THIS BOOK

In order to attempt to make the content of the Christian faith intelligible today, this book is divided into two major sections: fundamental topics and doctrinal topics. Part One examines a number of the basic aspects of Christianity, those dimensions of Christianity that ground everything else and upon which other dimensions depend if they are to be understood properly. It will accordingly discuss the nature of religious faith itself (what is a religious faith?); the idea of God (what do we mean by "God"?); revelation (what is revelation and why is it important?); Scripture and Tradition (what are they?); religion and religions (what do we mean by "religion" and how is Christianity related to other religions?); and finally religious language (what is the nature of and the problem with the kind of language religious traditions use?).

Part Two, on doctrinal topics, examines a number of key teachings of Christianity that are part of the Christian vision of reality. These have emerged as a result of the Christian claim that God has made God's self known in the interaction called revelation, particularly through Jesus of Nazareth. It will look, then, at the following: the world as created, the world as fallen, the world as redeemed through Jesus.

In connection with Jesus, there will be an examination of the new approach to understanding the source of our information about Jesus, the gospels, and the implications of this on how we might today understand Jesus as Lord and Savior. In this part a great deal of emphasis will be placed on the "Jesus of history," that is, on the Jesus who can be discovered by the application of scientific historical methods. What is meant by "scientific historical methods" will be explained, as will the importance of discovering the historical figure of Jesus.

NOTES

1. See the remarks of Jaroslav Pelikan in *The Christian Tradition: A History of the Development of Doctrine*, vol. 3: *The Growth of Medieval Theology (600-1300)* (Chicago: University of Chicago Press, 1978), pp. 255-267.

2. John Macquarrie, *Principles of Christian Theology*, 2nd edition (New York: Scribner's, 1977), p. 1.

QUESTIONS FOR REFLECTION AND DISCUSSION

1. Using the understanding of worldview outlined in the introduction, what are the elements of your worldview?

2. The recognition of the human dimension of Christianity is one of the features of the Copernican revolution in Christian thinking today. How do you understand what this means? What is your reaction to the statement?

3. How did you understand what theology is before reading this introduction? Has the introduction added to your understanding of it? Explain.

4. Make a list of what you think are the important elements of Christianity. Do any seem strange or unintelligible to you? Elaborate.

SUGGESTED READINGS

Hill, Brennan R., Paul Knitter, and William Madges. *Faith, Religion & Theology: A Contemporary Introduction*, chapter 9. Mystic, Conn.: Twenty-Third Publications, 1990.

Hodgson, Peter C., and Robert H. King, eds. *Christian Theology: An Introduction to Its Traditions and Tasks*. Revised edition. Philadelphia: Fortress Press, 1985. See pp. 1–28.

Macquarrie, John. *Principles of Christian Theology*. 2nd edition. New York: Charles Scribner's Sons, 1977. See pp. 1–20.

Rausch, Thomas P. *The College Student's Introduction to Theology*. Collegeville, Minn.: Liturgical Press. See chapter 1.

CHAPTER ONE

THE MEANING OF
RELIGIOUS FAITH

"**M**y geology professor insists that religious faith is at odds with modern science," a student recently stated, "because what the Bible says about creation is totally inconsistent with the scientific evidence." That is how a particular scientist reacts to the idea of religious faith. What about you? When you hear "religious faith," what comes to your mind? Do you think of churches or mosques, with people singing and praying? Does the image of a Bible or a crucifix come to mind? Or a statue of the Buddha? Perhaps you think of the emotional exhortations of a televangelist, or of someone whose religious faith has helped him or her through a crisis. Do you have a positive or a negative feeling when you hear these words? What do you think of?

The expression "religious faith" can bring many different images to our minds, so before we can examine the fundamental dimensions of the Christian faith we need to examine what a religious faith is really all about. Christianity is called, after all, a *religious* faith, and its followers are said to *have* a religious faith. What do we mean by this? What is it that characterizes a religious type of faith? And what other type of faith can we have, anyway?

All of us, in fact, have various forms of faith. Faith essentially involves trust or confidence in someone or something. We may trust—have faith in—a friend, for example, and by this we mean that our friend will not lie to us or desert us when we are in need of help. We may trust that existence is meaningful and good, so that when we comfort our children or an ailing friend by saying "Everything is all right," we have a confidence that it *is* all right. We may have a confidence in our worth and that of other persons. In all of this, we have a kind of faith, a basic trust or confidence.

A religious faith, however, involves more than this. In order to develop this, we should reflect on three experiences we have, experiences that inevitably provoke fundamental questions about our existence. It is how we find answers to these questions that leads to an understanding of what religious faith is. This way of approaching an understanding of religious faith will not only get at the essence of such faith, but will also show that religious faith relates very much to the most important questions we ask in our lives. The experiences we should look at that arouse these profound questions are: 1) the experience of the contingent nature of human existence, 2) the experience of a certain capacity for self-creation, and 3) the experience of distortion.

THREE EXPERIENCES AND THE QUESTIONS THEY PROVOKE

The experience of being contingent is perhaps one of the most thought-provoking experiences we can have. To understand this experience, let's meet June. She is an astronomer whose training has led her to see the universe as a vast, evolving "organism" in which stars and planets and galaxies have emerged out of a primordial "Big Bang." She is also familiar with the general shape of the emergence of life forms on Earth, various forms of life emerging from other forms of life in a long process that has resulted in the countless species of plants and animals, and ultimately the human race. She knows that she personally exists because of her parents. While she may not use the term, she also knows that all the things and forms of life and herself in this great cosmic process are *contingent*, that is, they depend on something or someone else for their existence. Philosophers will say that they are all *not necessary*; they need someone or something else for their coming into being.

June is struck at times by something more. She wonders occasionally, "What was the form of being before the Big Bang? Did the forces that caused it emerge out of something else? And if so, what caused this?" And sometimes she asks another question. "Does all of this coming into existence and going out of existence have any meaning? Why, for what purpose, is there this great cosmic flux? Why have I emerged out of all this?" June asks the questions, in other words: "Where have I (where has all this) come from, ultimately? What purpose is there to my existence, and that of everything else in the universe?" Simply put, she asks the questions of ultimate origins and of meaning. The experience of herself as contingent, and her realization that all else is likewise contingent has led her to ask these questions.

The second important experience we have, that of our self-creativity, likewise often leads us to ask profound questions. If you look at your own life, don't you experience a certain capacity for making yourself into a particular kind of person and for choosing particular types of activities? This capacity for "creating" your "self" is not an unlimited one. The human freedom to fashion a "self" is limited, even severely limited at times. Your genetic makeup, your historical and political environment, your age—all these factors and many more go into limiting the self you can fashion by your choices. Nonetheless, we humans do seem to have some measure of freedom.

But let's return to our astronomer, June. She has made decisions that have resulted in her particular career. She may, however, question this choice of career, even to the point of wondering if there is any real purpose to it. Is there any real meaning to her work as an astronomer? So what if she is able to observe the forces of the galaxy and make sense of them? Such a question is probably more common when a person is threatened by death. The thought of personal demise and the collapse of what one has been doing with one's life often triggers the concern to find meaning. "Has my life been worthwhile?" One can see this question pursued and answered in a pessimistic way by the writer of one of the books of the Bible, the Book of Ecclesiastes. The author writes:

Vanity of vanities, says the Teacher,
vanity of vanities! All is vanity.
What do people gain from all the toil
at which they toil under the sun? (Ecclesiastes 1:2–3)

Our capacity for making ourselves into particular persons raises this question of meaning: "Is there any meaning to the choices we make?" It also raises another question, the question of direction. Given that we have a limited capacity to make ourselves into particular persons, is there a particular direction that is better than another? For example, should I develop my self so that I am predominantly a caring person or a self-centered one? Why? Our capacity for self-creation raises the questions both of meaning and of direction.

The third important experience is what can be called distortion. As we grow up and become increasingly conscious of our world, we discover that this world, and our existence, is full of distortion. Something seems to be wrong. We experience animosity, hatred, and jealousy on both the personal and the social level. People argue and fight with one another; nations do the same thing. Exploitation and the resultant friction that this causes is rampant. Our attempts to dominate and control nature result in nature being thrown out of balance and striking back in the form of harmful, life-threatening pollution. Our astronomer, June, has experienced the preference given to some of her male colleagues when it comes to jobs. She senses that more is expected of her than of some of her male colleagues. She has experienced distortion in the form of what we call sexism. On many, many levels of our existence and in our activities, we experience this distortion and alienation. This causes us to ask at times, "Why is our existence like this?" And importantly, we ask, "Is there some way out of this situation?"

Where has the universe come from? Where, ultimately, have I come from? Why? Is there any purpose to the existence of all of this? To my existence? Why do I strive to create myself into a particular type of person? Does it make any difference how I do this? Why? Why is there so much alienation and distortion? Is there any relief from it? It is in the context of asking and answering these kinds of questions that one can approach an understanding of the essence of religious faith.

THE ESSENCE OF RELIGIOUS FAITH

When it comes to a *religious* faith, a trust or a confidence in someone or something that is religious, the idea of transcendence enters the picture. The term "transcendent" means "beyond." In the case at hand, it means first of all *beyond* or *other than* the world and its objects and forces and persons that we can experience by empirical means. Thus, we can see or measure objects like rocks or persons or trees, and we can measure forces such as the pull of gravity. We can also experience more subjective realities such as the love of a friend or a parent, or the beauty of a piece of music or of a painting.

But a religious faith involves more. A religious faith involves trust in a reality beyond and other than these. In relation to the experiences and the questions these provoke, which were discussed above, a religious faith involves trust in a transcendent reality that grounds or is the source of existence, meaning, and healing. The person with a religious faith, then, looks beyond the world and its forces in order to answer the question, "Where do I come from?" He or she has a trust, a confidence, in some transcendent reality that is the foundation of his or her existence and, indeed, the existence of the forces in the universe that have so interacted as to produce this universe. The person with a religious faith has a trust, a confidence, in a transcendent reality that grounds the assertion that *this* is the way to live, *this* is what counts as valuable in my life, and not that other. The person with a religious faith has a trust, a confidence, in a way out of the distortions he or she experiences in existence—in "salvation," in other words—that is based upon a transcendent force or power or reality.

The people who do not have a religious faith still seek answers to all these questions. But they do not find the answers coming from, or grounded in, a transcendent source. They try to find answers coming from themselves or from the world. Thus, they create or find answers with no reference to a transcendent reality, that is, with no reference to some reality beyond and other than themselves and the ordinary world of experience. Or, they do not find answers at all.

Secular humanism, a category that includes many groups of people, is a good example of this. One of the chief characteristics of secular humanists is that they are concerned with promoting and advancing human well-being. They do so with no reference to a transcendent reality, however. Humans, in this philosophy of life, determine for themselves what is good and worthwhile and meaningful. Humans work, by themselves, to identify and correct the distortions of human existence. The Greek philosopher Protagoras (c. 444 B.C.E.) summed up this approach very well when he said that humankind "is the measure of all things."[1] Humankind is the criterion and standard of truth.

Christian Tradition shows very well the reference to the transcendent that is characteristic of religious faith. In answer to the questions "Where do we come from?" and "Why is there a universe?" Christianity refers to what it calls "God." God is not one of the measurable forces or things of the universe, it insists, but is beyond and other than these. Christians also claim that it is possible to be freed from the distortions of existence and so they talk about salvation in this regard. And they look to God as the author of this salvation. Christians look, in other words, to a reality beyond themselves and their ordinary world of experience—to a reality called God—in order to answer life's most fundamental questions.

Essential to a religious faith, then, is this trustful reference to a transcendent source of existence, meaning, and healing. Whatever meaning there is to human life and to the cosmic processes depends on this transcendent reality, or power. The same is true for whatever healing is possible. Those who do not have a religious faith do not make this reference to transcendent reality.

But there is something more that is important for a proper understanding of a religious faith. The trustful confidence in some transcendent point of reference or ground of existence, meaning, and healing is accompanied by a *commitment* to this transcendent reality. *It* is experienced as being of ultimate worth and importance, as being supremely valuable. Trust in and commitment to this ultimate, transcendent reality are thus integral aspects of religious faith.

Religious faith, moreover, is not some vague, inarticulate trust and commitment. It takes concrete shape, in part, in and through *beliefs* or, better, a belief system. Beliefs result from the human attempt to say things about that ultimate, transcendent point of reference which is the object of religious faith. Beliefs result from the human attempt to say things about reality and human existence in light of this ultimate reality. This point will be developed later.

Religious faith is expressed in and through religious beliefs (not completely, however, because the way one acts is also an expression of faith). These beliefs arise as a result of experiences of the ultimate, transcendent ground of existence, meaning, and healing. The nature of these experiences will be the subject of Chapter Three, but before discussing that it is appropriate to reflect a little more on the intelligibility of this transcendent reality that is the ultimate point of reference for a religious faith.

Note
1. Quoted in Frederick Copleston, *A History of Philosophy*, Volume 1: *Greece & Rome*, Part 1, new revised edition (Garden City, N.Y.: Doubleday, 1962), p. 108.

Questions for Reflection and Discussion
1. Think about what came to your mind when you heard the expression "religious faith" before reading this chapter, and make a list of all that went into your understanding. Compare and/or contrast this with the suggestions of this chapter. When you finish reading this book, make the list again.

2. What is contingency? Reflect upon your own life. Have you experienced the sort of questions that June asked? If so, what was the context that triggered these questions? If not, do these questions make any sense to you? Explain.

3. Think about what you are doing now with your life. Does it have any meaning? Explain what meaning you see in your life. Do you answer that ultimately, it makes no difference whether one is a great statesman or a solitary drunkard?

4. List a number of negative features in your personal and community existence that you experience. Why do you consider them to be negative experiences? How do you account for them? Is there any remedy for them? Describe it.

SUGGESTED READINGS

Haight, Roger. *Dynamics of Theology*. Mahwah, N.J.: Paulist Press, 1990. See especially chapters 3, 4.

Hill, Brennan R., Paul Knitter, and William Madges. *Faith, Religion & Theology: A Contemporary Introduction*. Mystic, Conn.: Twenty-Third Publications, 1992. See especially chapters 1-4.

Macquarrie, John. *Principles of Christian Theology*. 2nd edition. New York: Charles Scribner's Sons, 1977. See especially chapter 3.

McBrien, Richard P. *Catholicism*. 2nd ed. San Francisco: HarperCollins, 1994. See chapter 2.

CHAPTER TWO

TOWARD AN
UNDERSTANDING OF GOD

Have you ever wondered how you could picture and talk about God or even whether you could justify belief in God? After all, have you ever seen or touched God? Has anyone you know ever done this? People who have religious faith, as noted in the previous chapter, claim that there *is* such a reality, although they cannot point to this reality as "over there" or "shake hands" with it. How might we reasonably talk about God? Is such talk reasonably justified? These are two important questions we have to address if Christianity is to make any sense at all.

THINKING ABOUT GOD

Thinking about or talking about God is very difficult, especially in our age, because we do not feel comfortable with "realities" we cannot measure or experience by means of our senses or by instruments we construct. In fact, we have a tendency to negate the reality of what is beyond empirical or scientific verification. An engineering student once told a classmate that she was crazy to be taking a theology course. "After all," he told her, "you can't prove all this stuff about God." What is more, our Western culture has become increasingly secular. It operates by and large without any meaningful reference to the Divine. As a result, the notion of God does not receive a lot of persistent reinforcement among us. Persons with a religious faith, then, confront the problem of how to think and talk about a "reality" that is not one of the measurable or observable forces, things, or persons of the universe. What is more, God does not seem to be "doing" anything that receives any press.

One approach toward understanding the reality we call God was mentioned in Chapter One: God as the *ground* of existence, meaning, and healing. God is not one of the things or forces or persons of our ordinary world, but is rather the ground and source of all these, giving them meaning. "Ground" is a word used to deal with the affirmation that God is indeed a reality, but one totally unlike the realities we normally "bump into." And this is crucial for any understanding of God that is true to our experience: we must find a way of thinking and talking about God that deals with the difference between God and all the things, forces, or persons of "ordinary" experience, yet at the same time indicates that there is real substance to the reality we are talking about.

Along these lines, some theologians talk about God as Being Itself, as distinct from the beings that make up our normal world of experience. For example, John Macquarrie, whose understanding of theology we have already seen, uses this terminology, describing God (Being) as the "incomparable that lets-be." God is not a being, but rather the "letting-be" of all beings, that which enables them to stand out of nothingness.[1]

Yet another approach toward understanding what we mean by "God" appears in the writings of those who follow what is called the "transcendental" approach to God.[2] These writers reflect upon the nature of our capacity to know and to will. Thus, in this approach, we humans are seekers of knowledge who desire to know more and more. We come to a knowledge of something, yet we are aware that there is always *more*. Our knowledge has limits and we continually strive to go beyond these limits and search for what we do not yet know. Those who adopt a transcendental approach to understanding human activity ask, in this light, "Why do we realize that our knowing is limited?" Their answer is that we only know this if we are aware of "more," something beyond our present knowledge. It is like being aware of a fence or a boundary. How do we recognize something as a boundary unless we are aware of something beyond the boundary? Only in light of an awareness of something more can we recognize that anything has a limit. Now, the quest to know seems to be unlimited or infinite. We *always* seem aware of the limits of our knowing, that "something more" can be known. This implies that we are aware of the "Infinite," in comparison with which we recognize all else as limited and finite.

The awareness of the Infinite is not a direct awareness, but rather is an implicit awareness, a background awareness, through which we are directly aware of things. Rather than being a direct awareness of something there, like our awareness of that tree over there in our yard, it is more like the awareness we have of the sunlight by virtue of which we see that tree. This Infinite, then, serves as a kind of horizon or backdrop awareness to our quest to know. We are "aware" of it not as the direct object of our consciousness, but as the condition for our experience that there is "more."

The same type of thinking applies to our longings. We desire more and more. We want to possess more things; we desire to love and be loved. We want to be powerful. On many levels, we want to have or to be. Yet we find ourselves always unsatisfied; we always want more. No finite thing or person can satisfy us. We continually reach out for the Infinite. In her novel, *A City of Bells*, Elizabeth Goudge captures this infinite longing and dissatisfaction that is part of the human experience: ". . . human longing is too vast a thing to be satisfied by anything that the earth holds; human love, like natural beauty, can comfort but it cannot satisfy."[3]

Do we reach out to infinite nothingness or infinite fullness? Is the "infinite" nothing, or is it a positive reality that beckons us and surrounds us? Those who believe in God, who adopt this approach, talk about God as that infinite "Mystery" that surrounds us in light, of which we know and which we strive after. God is that "Infinite" we constantly reach out for.

Does God Exist?

So far in this chapter we have centered on ways of thinking about God. But because of the elusiveness of God, because God "cannot be measured on the Richter scale," what gives us the right to affirm that there is such a reality? Does God really exist? A fruitful approach to this overriding question is to reflect upon our basic confidence in the ultimate trustworthiness of existence. In order to develop this, let us consider once again the experience of our contingency.[4]

Through the experience of our contingency, as noted in the preceding chapter, we come to the realization that we are "not necessary," that is, we do not exist in and of ourselves. Rather, our existence is a dependent one. We depend for existence on our parents. Indeed, we and they and all persons, animals, and things come into existence in the context of a marvelous and lengthy series of interactions that make up the cosmic processes. Given this context, it is natural to ask: are we the products of a cosmic sea that churns inexorably on, generating stars and solar systems and forces and energies and me—all of this simply happening? Or is there something more? Are we part of a series of cosmic processes that have a ground beyond the processes themselves and that give these processes and my emerging in them some purpose, some meaning? To put it another way: are we like driftwood randomly thrown up onto the shore from a churning cosmic sea, or are we like thoughtful words uttered by some gracious source? The choices boil down to these two, and these two alone, in the final analysis. There is no third option. But this does not prove that there is or must be a gracious source to the cosmic processes that gives these processes meaning. It simply says that there are two alternatives from which we must choose. How do we know which choice to make?

There is no easy answer to this question, either way. We must make an act of faith about this most essential of all questions and decide without completely compelling logical or empirical proof. This does not mean, though, that the decision is like tossing a coin into the air and deciding on the basis of whether it comes down heads or tails. We have "indications," or experiences, that point us in the direction of affirming the "reality" of a gracious ground of existence. One such experience is our implicit sense of meaning that allows us to trust in the worthwhileness of our existence. Most people go through life assuming that their existence and that of other human beings is meaningful. What they do is not for nothing; it is not meaningless. The question is: does this implicit sense of meaning have a basis, a ground? Or is it an illusion, a kind of defense mechanism we build up around our lives to protect us from the awful realization that existence has no meaning? The sense of meaningfulness is there; what is its source?

If this sense that our existence is meaningful *has* a basis in reality, what is this basis? Can the universe, the things in it, and the processes that move the universe ground this sense of meaning? We may look at the stars and the planets and discover the forces that interact to form them. As we look at them, we may ask, "Do these give us the assurance that the cosmic processes have meaning, that 'everything is all right' and that our existence is good and trustworthy?" Our response would have to be that the universe itself is incapable of grounding the implicit feeling of meaning most humans have. It does not appear capable of assuring us in a positive way that "everything is all right." This means that if there is to be a ground in reality for the feeling of meaningfulness we have, if this feeling is not based on an illusion, it must be based on something "outside" the universe. It must have its ground in a reality "other" than the stars and planets and forces we can experience. And this transcendent ground of meaning is one way of understanding what we mean by God.

This is certainly not a proof in the sense of being empirically verifiable or capable of being logically deduced in an absolutely compelling way. What is important, though, is that it provides a justifiable basis for affirming the "existence" of a reality called God. It requires an act of faith, to be sure, but this act of faith does not appear unreasonable. It is an act of faith that our experience of meaning tells us the truth about ourselves, and since the universe and its entities and forces cannot justify this experience, we must look beyond. It is not, then, a matter simply of flipping a coin in the air and deciding on the basis of which side comes up. Nor is belief in God superstitious or an outmoded throwback to a time when people did not really understand their world and its forces. It is based on questions about the source or the ground of the sense of meaning we experience.

Notes

1. See Macquarrie, *Principles of Christian Theology*, ch. 5.

2. One of the most influential Roman Catholic twentieth-century theologians to develop this approach towards understanding God is Karl Rahner. For an introduction to his approach, see J. Norman King, *Experiencing God All Ways and Every Day* (Minneapolis: Winston, 1982).

3. Elizabeth Goudge, *A City of Bells* (London: Hodder and Stoughton; Coronet Books), p. 244.

4. This approach is developed in Hans Küng, *Does God Exist? An Answer for Today*, translated by Edward Quinn (Garden City, N.Y.: Doubleday, 1980). See especially pp. 552-584.

Questions for Reflection and Discussion

1. Try to recall the ways you understood "God" before reading this chapter. Make a list. Compare or contrast this list with what you have read here.

2. Explain the argument of this chapter that only if God exists can our sense of meaning be trusted.

3. Do you believe in God? Do you not believe in God? In either case, explain why.

4. Explain why this chapter has argued that a term such as "ground" is an appropriate term for God.

SUGGESTED READINGS

Berger, Peter. *A Rumor of Angels: Modern Society and the Rediscovery of the Supernatural.* Garden City, N.Y.: Doubleday, 1970.

Hick, John. *Philosophy of Religion.* 3rd edition. Englewood Cliffs, N.J.: Prentice-Hall, 1983. See especially chapters 2 and 3.

King, J. Norman. *Experiencing God All Ways and Every Day.* Minneapolis: Winston Press, 1982.

McFague, Sallie. *The Body of God: An Ecological Theology.* Minneapolis: Augsburg Fortress, 1993.

CHAPTER THREE

REVELATION

W hat is the meaning of my life? Where have I come from? What is my destiny? What is right and what is wrong? Why is there suffering? What awaits me after death? These are among the important questions that our existence provokes us to ask. But where do we find answers? The Christian faith says that we find the answers to these questions through revelation, a word that has the root meaning of "unveiling." Moreover, according to Christianity, through revelation we not only find answers to these questions, we also learn more about the ultimate reality we name "God." The content of the Christian faith—that is, its understanding of God and the world and human existence—depends on revelation, then. Well, what sort of experience is revelation? How are we to think about it? It is this dimension of the Christian faith that we will now begin to explore.

RELIGIOUS EXPERIENCE

We can come to an understanding of revelation by relating it to religious experience. When asked in class what comes to mind when they hear "religious experience," students offer a variety of responses. Some think of apparitions of the Blessed Virgin Mary. Others speak of the Christian sacraments or attending Mass or being at an evangelical revivalist meeting. What do you think of?

Here is one woman's religious experience. When she was in grade school, an unexpected and unforgettable thing happened at a Christmas concert. A young man, widely made fun of because of his slowness of mind and obesity, stood up to sing. The woman says that music has always been a way for her to come in contact with beauty, but when she heard this large man begin to sing, she was brought beyond the mere beauty of the musical structure and the words, right into a starlit sky, into the presence of angels and shepherds. She was really there, present in the stable at that first Christmas. She was transported from the small church where the concert took place into a time when God came to dwell among us. When the man stopped singing, the woman says she felt an incredible peace and a sense of the Holy. She has been able to recall and relive this experience ever since. The young man was, for her, truly a God-bearer. That night, she truly experienced the presence and the reality of God.

A religious experience is essentially an experience of the Divine. Let us set aside the question of whether such experiences are "true," for the moment, and reflect upon their structure. Key to understanding religious experience is the notion of *depth*: the Divine is experienced as a depth dimension of some person, thing, or event. We all experience various persons, things, or events around us, every day and all of our waking moments. We see trees; we hear a cat meowing; we are aware that our sister is in the next room listening to her radio; we look through a microscope and discover the tiny world of bacteria; we are aware of wars and famines around the world. But there are also times when such experiences involve the experience of "something more." This is not an experience outside our awareness of a person, thing, or event, but is rather co-experienced in and through or along with it. It involves such realities as meaning, value, or beauty.

Here is an example. A number of years ago, there was a popular movie called *Gandhi*. It was the story of the great Hindu leader, Mohandas Gandhi, one of the founding figures of modern India who was a leading crusader of Indian independence from England. As people watched the life of Gandhi on the screen, some were seized by the conviction that, yes, this is how to live! The values and attitudes that dominated Gandhi's life confronted them in a powerful way, such that they knew a truly authentic human life must include these values. They were brought into contact with this man and the values that he lived, and they were seized by a call to "be like that." There was, in other words, another dimension to their experience of Gandhi—there was a depth experience.

Other examples abound. Listening to a Beethoven string quartet might evoke, for some, the enthralling reaction that "this is beautiful."

Negative forms of depth experience are possible, too. We can be deeply moved as we experience life as meaningless, or we can experience someone's life as "undesirable," a life we do not want to imitate.

A depth experience, then, is the experience of something or someone, *but also* in and through that something beyond, "something more," such as truth, beauty, or meaning. This "something more" is part of the overall experience, and when it involves the Divine, or God, in some way, then we enter the realm of religious experience. Religious experience can thus be defined as the experience of the Divine, of some ultimate, transcendent presence or power that occurs in and through the experience of a person, thing, or event as a depth dimension to that "ordinary" experience.

REVELATION

What has just been said about religious experience helps us understand that important dimension of the Christian faith called revelation. This is because revelation is a type of religious experience. Some religious experiences have been so attractive and have had such power in eliciting responses from large numbers of people that religious communities have grown up and developed as a result of them. These powerful, attractive experiences of the Divine that stand at the base of religious traditions constitute revelation. These experiences are crucial. Because of them the religious traditions concerned say what they do about the Divine and about the meaning and destiny of human existence. In the case of Christianity, what it says about God, what it says about the proper relationship between God and human beings and between humans themselves, and what it says about the very meaning and goal of human existence—all of this is the result of profound encounters with God. In other words, the wisdom that Christianity possesses emerges out of revelation. Revelation is truly a fundamental dimension of the Christian faith!

CHRISTIAN REVELATION

Christian Tradition is based on a number of particular experiences of the Divine, experiences involving a series of historical events and the life and person of an historical figure. These constitute the media in and through which revelation occurs. The events in question are, first, the formation of the people of Israel to which that body of writing we call the Old Testament, or Hebrew Scriptures, gives witness. Christians and Jews claim that God has disclosed the Divine Self and has revealed to humans what life is really all about and, further, has offered salvation or healing to humans in and through the historical events connected with the formation of the people of Israel. So, when the Hebrew people remembered the migration of their original ancestors, Abraham and Sarah, from their homeland to the land of Palestine, the Hebrew people understood this migration to be a result of God's call to Abraham and Sarah to do so and God's promise to them that they would be ancestors of a great nation. Their migration had a religious dimension to it. When Jeremiah witnessed the defeat of Jerusalem by Nebuchadnezzar in 588 B.C.E., he experienced God's hand at work there, punishing the Israelites for their lack of faithfulness to God. These events, with their divine depth, are but two such revelatory experiences upon which Judaism is based. For Christians, however, the definitive, unsurpassable encounter with the Divine is that encounter with the Divine in and through the life and person of Jesus of Nazareth. God was experienced in this man and his life. His was not merely a human life. His words and values were more than human. And this encounter is the source of the Christian movement.

HUMAN DIMENSION OF REVELATION

The introduction to this book claimed that significant changes have occurred in the way Christians understand things today, such that a Copernican revolution is taking place. Revelation is one of the many areas where a new awareness is affecting our outlook and approach to religion. The essence of this new awareness is that we are now aware more than ever of the human dimension of revelation. For Christians of past ages, revelation was an experience of God in which God exerted all the influence. What Christianity said about God or human existence came, literally, from God. God, of course, had to reveal things in a way we could understand, and so God used human words and ideas. But the emphasis was on God's activity.

During this century, however, a very different approach has taken hold. Christian thinkers, for the most part, now take it for granted that human beings condition any experience of the Divine. What a person says or thinks as a result of experiencing God—indeed, the very way a person experiences God—is conditioned by the worldview the person has. The person actively shapes the experience.

To elaborate on this idea of the conditioning, interpretive role the humans involved in a revelatory experience play, consider the pictures on page 26. When you look at them, what do you see?

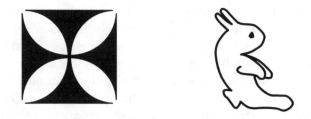

You may see something different than what your friend sees. Indeed, people see different things in these pictures. In one classroom situation, some students saw an iron cross in the first drawing; others saw the petals of a flower. Some saw a rabbit in the second, others a duck. Still others might see something else. The point is that the experience, what was "seen," was not simply a function of the drawings themselves, but also of the persons looking at them. They played a shaping role in the total experience. We might engage in lengthy social and psychological analyses to determine why one student "saw" one thing rather than another, but the key point is that the experience depends, to some extent, on the person having the experience. What we experience is not simply a function of the reality "out there," but is also a function of our interpretive minds.

The interpretive, conditioning role of persons involved in a revelatory experience is a function of the particular culture in which they live. We are all born into a particular culture. If you consider what a person's culture does, you will see that it provides the various "filters" through which reality is experienced, understood, and talked about. For example, in the cultural worldview of our Christian forebears, the world was composed of stable, unchanging substances. There were rocks, trees, plants, and animals, and these were all made—as is—during the six "days" of creation. In our present way of understanding reality, we use the notion of evolution. We perceive things around us as having developed from prior entities, over vast periods of time, as the forces of the cosmos interact. Change and process characterize our present-day understanding of reality. Our culture, moreover, provides us with ways of understanding what the meaning of existence is, or what counts in life. It provides us with a way of arriving at the truth, with interpretive categories for understanding our world, and with a language to use in order to talk about our world and share our experiences with others. In all these ways, and many more, our culture provides us with the interpretive filters through which reality is perceived, understood, and described.

What has this to do with revelation? A great deal! The cultural "filters" through which we experience, understand, and describe reality will play a role in any experience of God. Our experience of the Divine does not depend solely on the Divine coming into our history and into our consciousness any more than what you experienced when you looked at the pictures on the preceding page depended solely on the pictures themselves. The experience of the Divine also depends on the persons experiencing the Divine who shape that experience. Like a prism, the "filters" of our culture through which we see reality refract our experience of the Divine.

Revelatory experiences, then, do not simply involve God's breaking into human history; they also involve the human response to this inbreaking and the human perception of it. This does not mean, it is important to note, that the human recipient of a revelatory situation determines completely what is experienced. God's breaking into human history also shapes the experience. The recipient, for example, may feel that his or her present language is not capable of describing and interpreting the experience completely or adequately. Thus he or she may be forced to find a new way of speaking or twist current language so that it may more closely approach an understanding of the experience. Yet, this attempt to find a new language and the new way of perceiving reality that is inevitably the result of revelation will bear the stamp of the recipient's culture. From his or her cultural setting, she or he will struggle to find a way of expressing and understanding the experience. There is a dialectical relationship in any revelatory experience: the inbreaking of the Divine is conditioned by the human recipients, and this experience affects their perception of things and calls them to see things anew.

REVELATION IN RECENT ROMAN CATHOLIC REFLECTION

In order to glimpse something of the discussion going on in Christian circles about revelation, it would be useful to look at what the Roman Catholic tradition has said about it during the course of this century. This examination will not only show what a major Christian denomination says about revelation, but it will set the stage for an examination of the two topics that will follow this one, Scripture and Tradition.

The discussion that follows will focus on two important ecumenical councils of the Catholic church and what they said about revelation: the First Vatican Council (1870) and the Second Vatican Council (1962-1965). The first council set the parameters for Catholic thinking about revelation for the first half of the present century; the second introduced a different approach, which has determined Catholic thinking in the second half.

For the most part, the First Vatican Council adopted a "propositional" approach in its understanding of revelation. In this view, revelation is the communication to humans by God of a series of "propositions," or statements, that humans are called on to believe because God has revealed them. For the bishops at that council, these truths could be either "natural" truths or "supernatural" truths. Natural truths were those truths that human beings could discern by their reasoning powers or by observation. For example, human beings could come to the knowledge of the truth that Earth revolved around the sun, or that the whole is greater than its parts, and so on. But for Catholic theology at this time, there were also "supernatural" truths, which God revealed to humans. These were beyond the ability of human reasoning to know or discover. They had, quite literally, to be revealed by God. God, through inspiration, made these truths known to certain people who passed them on. An example was the doctrine of the Trinity, which means that God's essence involved three "persons" sharing equally one "nature."

Revelation, then, was the communication to us, by inspiration, of a number of truths. These revealed to us what God was like and, importantly, how we humans ought to live and how we attained salvation. Seen from another perspective, revelation was the entire collection of these truths. Thus, one sees terminology such as the "deposit" of revelation.

In Roman Catholic thinking during the first half of this century, these truths could be found in the Bible and in the church's Tradition. The Bible, therefore, was seen primarily as a collection of inspired truths that God had made known to us, revealing to us the divine nature and God's plan of salvation for us. The Tradition of the Roman Catholic church was seen as those truths that the church, led by God's Spirit, deduced from the biblical truths, or those truths that were revealed to the early church through the inspiration of the Holy Spirit. That children should be baptized, for example, or that Mary should be venerated, are examples of this latter. Many Protestants held to this general view of revelation, but they tended to restrict the place where revealed truths may be found to the Bible.

While not denying that in the process called revelation humans are put in touch with certain truths, the Second Vatican Council took a different tack. Rather than see revelation primarily as the communication to us of truths, it saw revelation in terms of a personal encounter between humans and God, in which God comes to meet human beings as friends, calling them into communion with the Divine Self, offering them salvation. A key section from the statement on revelation of the Second Vatican Council reads as follows:

> It pleased God, in his goodness and wisdom, to reveal himself and to make known the mystery of his will (see Ephesians 1:9). His will was that [human beings] should have access to the Father, through Christ, the Word made flesh, in the Holy Spirit, and thus become sharers in the divine nature (see Ephesians 2:18; 2 Peter 1:4). By this revelation, then, the invisible God (see Colossians 1:15; 1 Timothy 1:17), from the fullness of his love, addresses [human beings] as his friends (see Exodus 33:11; John 15:14-15), and moves among them (see Baruch 3:38), in order to invite and receive them into his own company.[1]

The latter approach is more in line with the view sketched out earlier, where revelation was described in terms of an encounter with the Divine. Out of this encounter, humans perceive certain "truths," that is, they claim to understand such things as what reality is all about, something about the nature of the Divine, what really matters in life, and so forth. Unlike the propositional understanding of revelation, this approach lends itself to recognizing the human conditioning of these truths. These truths do not come "from God" as if they dropped down from heaven into human minds. Rather, they emerge out of the attempts by human beings to express their understanding of this encounter with the Divine. The implications of this approach on understanding the Bible and the Tradition of the church will become apparent in the next two chapters.

ONE REVELATION OR MANY? THE PROBLEM OF VERIFICATION

In what has been said so far, the possibility has been left open that there are a number of revelations, that is, a number of powerful, attractive encounters between human beings and God. The question arises,

How do we know if a particular claim of experiencing God is valid? After all, Muhammad claimed that he had encountered God. So did Moses. So did the great Christian missionary Paul, whose letters make up part of the Christian Scriptures. Did all these people really encounter the Divine breaking into their lives? The problem with these claims, and indeed all the claims of religious experiences, is that they are based on depth experiences, encounters with the Divine in and through some other experience. And we cannot empirically verify them. We cannot, for example, measure depth experiences such as beauty on a machine. What we can say is that a person claims to experience beauty. The same holds true for revelatory experiences.

What is more, not everyone experiencing the same person, event, or thing has this depth experience of the Transcendent. That is fundamental for revelation. The Roman soldiers looking at Jesus on the cross, for example, saw a troublemaker. Some of Jesus' followers, reflecting on the same event, "saw," or experienced, something else—namely, the saving power of God. The same event was interpreted in different ways by different people. One has to face, then, the problem of verification of claims regarding revelatory experiences.

A fruitful direction in dealing with this problem is to say that valid revelatory experiences will be *self-authenticating* over the long haul. The experience, if it truly is an encounter with the Divine, that transcendent ground of meaning and healing, will have the power of eliciting a responsive chord within people such that they will find their lives more meaningful and will experience what it is to live authentically. And it will have the power to do this for generations; it will have a truly lasting power. This is, of course, no real "proof" in the sense of a logical or scientific proof. But it is a kind of existential, lived proof.

This opens up the possibility of a variety of real revelatory experiences in the world. Are all of them equally valid? Does it matter upon which one a person bases his or her life? How are they all related to one another? These are questions that will be taken up in a later chapter of this section on fundamental themes, a chapter dealing with the meaning of religion and the relationship between the various religions of the world. But before doing that, we must look at two chapters closely related to revelation: Scripture and Tradition.

Note

1. "The Dogmatic Constitution on Divine Revelation" in *Vatican Council II: The Conciliar and Post Conciliar Documents,* new revised edition (Northport, N.Y.:

Costello, 1984), article 2. I have changed the exclusive word "men" to "human beings."

QUESTIONS TO FOR REFLECTION AND DISCUSSION

1. What is a depth experience? Can you identify any such experience from your own life? Elaborate.

2. Do you know anyone who has claimed to have had a religious experience? If so, describe it. What did that person say about it? What was your reaction to what was described?

3. Did the term "revelation" mean anything to you before reading this chapter? Elaborate. Has this chapter added anything to your understanding of revelation?

4. Discuss what this chapter says about the human dimension of revelation. Does this have any implication for understanding claims of experiencing God?

SUGGESTED READINGS

Dulles, Avery. *Models of Revelation.* Garden City, N.Y.: Doubleday, 1983.

Hick, John. *Philosophy of Religion.* 3rd edition. Englewood Cliffs, N.J.: Prentice-Hall, 1983. See especially chapter 5.

Lane, Dermot. *The Experience of God: An Invitation to Do Theology.* Mahwah, N.J.: Paulist Press, 1981.

Rausch, Thomas P. *The College Student's Introduction to Theology.* Collegeville, Minn.: Liturgical Press, 1993. See especially chapter 5.

CHAPTER FOUR

SCRIPTURE

A t the beginning of Chapter One, there was a reference to a geology professor who judged religious faith suspect because what the Bible said about creation was inconsistent with the scientific data on evolution. For him, one believed science or the Bible. And there is no doubt which of the two he believed. Nor is there any doubt about what some evangelicals believe. The Bible for them is inerrant, the ultimate criterion of all truth and it judges science. Science is wrong if it contradicts the Bible.

What do you think? When you think of the Bible, what comes to your mind? Is it God's Word? Is it a book of absolute and infallible truths? Is it an odd book that talks about a world different from the world of our everyday experience, a world of miracles and supernatural events? Is it a book of unbelievable myths? These kinds of varied reactions are common. It is now time to talk about the nature of the Bible and its importance in the Christian faith.

The Bible constitutes Scripture for Christians. Scripture is a word derived from the Latin word *scriptura*, which means "a piece of writing." For Christians, though, the Bible is not just any piece of writing. It is a privileged, authoritative piece of writing. Actually, it is more accurate to say that the Bible is a special, authoritative *collection* of writings, since it contains many different types of literature written by many different authors over a long period of time. What is so special about the Bible? Why is it authoritative? These are questions we will now address.

TOWARD AN UNDERSTANDING OF SCRIPTURE

A proper understanding of the Bible, or Scripture, must begin with a reminder about revelation. At the base of religions such as Judaism, Islam, and Christianity, stand powerful revelatory experiences, or at least claims of such experiences. An awareness of the Divine has seized certain people, and this has set off a chain of events from which these religions have emerged.

One of the things that happens, or can happen, when such encounters with the Divine take place is that people talk about them and they write about them. They try to describe the experience, or understand it, or draw out its implications for their lives. A body of writing can emerge because of such encounters, writing that claims to describe or understand or reflect on them. The writing resulting from revelatory experiences is the basis for what we call Scripture.

Indeed, in the case of Judaism and Christianity, writings did emerge as a result of an encounter with the Divine. Some of this writing came to be accepted as authentically witnessing to or interpreting these experiences. A basic definition of the Christian Bible, or Scripture, is this: *Scripture is that body of writing that has been accepted by the Christian community as being the authentic witness to, and interpretation of, Christianity's foundational revelation.* Seen in this way, Scripture is not itself revelation; it witnesses to revelation or comments on it. In the Christian Tradition, then, we see in the Bible, first, the accepted written witness to the God experienced in the formation and development of the people of Israel, which is the dominant theme or story of the Old Testament. Second, we see the written witness to the God experienced in and through the life and person of Jesus of Nazareth. This, and reflection on the meaning of this experience, is what the New Testament is all about.

It is important to realize that when it comes to the Christian Scriptures, the believing communities of the early church played a determining role in their makeup. The early Christian communities accepted the Jewish Scriptures as Scripture for themselves. They also determined which of the writings concerning Jesus and the Christian life should be counted as "canonical," that is, as acceptable. It was they who accepted the Jewish Scriptures, comprising roughly what we today call the Old Testament, as "Scripture." It is simply not the case that there first was Scripture and then there was a church. First came the church, the community of believers; then Scripture emerged from that community as it reflected on those foundational experiences of the Divine that lay at its origins. The church determined what was to be accepted as Scripture and what was not. And the process of determination continued for centuries.

One can see lists of acceptable writings being proposed into the third century C.E. and even into the sixteenth century. One of the arguments between Reformer Martin Luther and the Catholic church was about which books were authentically part of the canon of Scripture. Even today, Protestants and Roman Catholics disagree on what is truly Scripture. The Catholic community accepts as Scripture a number of Old Testament writings that the Protestant traditions call "apocryphal," that is, of doubtful authenticity. If you open one of the new ecumenical translations of the Bible, such as the New American Bible or the New Revised Standard Version of the Bible, you will see these "disputed" books included in a separate section.

Scripture plays a twofold role in the Christian community. First of all, it mediates the foundational revelation that stands at the source of Christianity to those who cannot have this actual foundational revelatory experience. Christians claim that God was at work in and through the life of Jesus of Nazareth. But we today do not have direct contact with this man and his life. How do we have access to the experience of those who did? We do so through Scripture. Second, Scripture functions as a norm and guide for the Christian community. Once a particular group of writings or a piece of writing has been accepted as Scripture, then everything else the religious community involved says and does is to be guided by or controlled by what Scripture says. Scripture is, after all, the authentic witness to that community's foundational revelation. The thought and practice of the community develops with constant reference to its Scripture.

HUMAN DIMENSION OF SCRIPTURE

Perhaps the most significant aspect of a proper understanding of Scripture today, a dimension of Scripture which is part of the Copernican revolution that is taking place in contemporary Christian theology, is the human dimension of Scripture. This dimension of Scripture has profound implications on how Scripture is understood, how it is used, and on two related theological topics, namely, the inerrancy and the inspiration of Scripture.

It is not too much of a caricature to say that for most of Christian history and for many people today, Scripture was (is) virtually or quite literally the *Word of God*: the Bible contains *God's* words and thoughts, those words and thoughts that *God* wanted to reveal to human beings for the sake of their salvation. The emphasis is so much on the Bible as *God's* word that it was easy to make the jump to the idea that the Bible is *inerrant*, that is, without error of any kind. It had to be, it was maintained; God could not lie. Indeed, this is the dominant view of that group of Christians called fundamentalists in North America, or sometimes evangelicals. So, if the Bible says that God created the world and everything in it in six days, that is how the world came into being, despite what the sciences say. These sciences are quite simply wrong because they contradict the very Word of God. This attitude undergirds the attempts on the part of literalists to prove the historical accuracy of the Bible and its scientific correctness in every detail. The search for Noah's ark is one example of such an attempt.

This fundamentalist approach toward understanding the biblical texts is one that mainstream, academic Christian theology—and indeed, many of the traditional Christian denominations—quite simply do not use today. Instead, we see another approach, one that assumes that the Bible was written by human beings, that it is thoroughly, through and through, *human*. One cannot separate a supposedly divine word from a human word as one would separate the layers of an onion. Scripture is a collection of human writings.

If we adopt this approach, which recognizes the profound humanity of Scripture, then we have to say that the Bible, written by humans, will reflect the historical, cultural situation of its human authors, and, what is more, *all* their humanity with all its foibles and greatness. We then have to admit the possibility of mistakes, of the authors not knowing things, of relying on incomplete or false sources, and even of what we call today ideology, that is, writing so that a particular point of view, a particular worldview, is advanced. One also has to admit the possibility of pettiness as well as greatness on the part of the authors. The biblical writings will reflect human nature and the human condition in what they say. That is why the Bible can seem so "funny" to us today. Its writings reflect views of reality that are "premodern," views of reality that come from cultures that are very old. Thus, it should not be surprising that the Bible reflects no awareness of such things as, for example, what we call "evolution." This view of reality is quite recent in terms of human knowledge; it could not possibly have been held when the biblical texts were written.

What were the humans who wrote the Jewish and Christian Scriptures trying to say? As already noted, we could say that they were trying to describe or interpret or comment upon God as God was encountered, first of all in the formation of the people of Israel (in the case of the Old Testament), and as God was experienced in and through the life and person of Jesus of Nazareth (in the case of the New Testament). To put it another way, Scripture is the result of the human attempts to deal with those powerful revelatory experiences that stand at the very base of the Judaeo-Christian religious Tradition.

WORD OF GOD, INERRANCY, INSPIRATION

What can we do with the traditional Christian affirmation that the Bible is the Word of God if one adopts with seriousness the human dimension of Scripture? Perhaps the best thing to do is to rephrase what we Christians hold: the Bible is the human Word of God. All parts of this expression have to be taken seriously. What this means is that in and through the very human words of Scripture, the voice of God, as it were, addresses us. We do not, then, encounter merely human words and human ideas. We encounter in and through these human words and ideas God's word and will for us. These human words and ideas become symbols of God for us in the sense that they mediate to us the reality of the Divine.

In this understanding of Scripture, what is meant by the terms "inerrancy" and "inspiration" has to be rethought. The Bible is not, literally, "without error" in the sense that what it says about scientific matters and historical events must be true. The biblical authors shared, in many ways, the general understanding of the world that their contemporaries shared; they were not privy to any special information in those premodern times about atoms or molecules or the forces of evolution. They were subject to faulty or incomplete sources in their historical accounts. They were subject to their enthusiasm and their biases. They cannot be faulted for not knowing about the development of the cosmos, as we do today; they cannot be faulted if they did not have access to all the historical records we might deem useful. They may be faulted if they willfully distorted, for their own glory and ends, the story they were writing. To call what they wrote "inerrant," though, is misleading and so this is one of those terms that is best left to slip away into the past, a reflection of a particular way of understanding the Bible based upon the presupposition that it came literally from God with little human input. When it comes to "inspiration," however, perhaps there is a way of understanding the term that is useful for us today and consistent with understanding the Bible as the human Word of God.

All too often, the term "inspiration" means God's influence on the authors of Scripture such that they became like secretaries, simply taking dictation from God. Their role in the process of the writing of Scripture and indeed the role of the community in which they lived are thus minimized, if not negated. But looked at in another way, we can say that at the very basis of the term is the idea that God is involved in the development and writing of the biblical material. These writings are not purely and simply human. At the very least, they emerged as humans reflected on and wrote about profound experiences *of the Divine*, experiences that they had themselves or that the Tradition of their community passed on to them. God was experienced as breaking into human history, and this is what the writings in the Bible talk about. Understanding "inspiration" in this way takes seriously into account that the Bible is the human word of God.

AUTHORITY OF SCRIPTURE

What can one say about the authority of Scripture? In the past, when Scripture was understood quite literally to be the "word of God," it was easy to acknowledge it as supremely authoritative. It was God's Word and so it had the highest authority possible! But as the human Word of God, can the Bible have any authority? Here again, we must take a new approach. The Bible is indeed authoritative. Its authority though, lies not in its being the absolute, literal word of God, but rather in its ability to mediate to us "something" of the Transcendent, that is, in its ability to put us in touch with the Divine. The authority lies, furthermore, in its special character as a kind of "constitution" for the Christian communities.

Some writings have the ability to put us in touch with profound truths about reality, even writings coming from different times and different cultures than our own. These may be called "classic" texts. When reading them, many people recognize that they are being confronted by some truth or truths about themselves or about their existence. For example, Charles Dickens's *A Christmas Carol* might be one of these. Upon reading this piece of fictional narrative, one may be seized by an awareness, like Ebenezer Scrooge in the story, of what it means to lead an authentic human existence, what attitudes and values truly count. So, generosity as characterisitic of an authentic human life can seize us as this story is read. The Bible may be thought of in this way, as a kind of "religious classic." It has the power of putting us in touch with the Divine in and through its human words and human thoughts, and this despite its premodern worldview. Here again, the notion of self-authenticity emerges. Many people (not all) "feel" or "experience" the reality of God in and through Scripture. It seems to have this "power" of eliciting a responsive chord from people and calling them to "see" reality and their existence in new ways and with reference to God.

The Bible is also a kind of "constitution" for Christians. A constitution sets forth the basic spirit and values of a society. It is always re-examined and interpreted anew as a community confronts new situations and new questions, but the constitution points the community in a particular direction. As the Christian constitution, the Bible occupies a privileged place as setting the direction and the values that ought to dominate the Christian movement. But as an historically conditioned document, reflecting the limits of its human authors, it is subject to interpretation as Christian communities try to apply its insights to their current situation.

THE HERMENEUTICAL QUESTION

This last remark raises the "hermeneutical" question. Hermeneutics means interpretation. In the context of this chapter it has to do with interpreting Scripture. The most important hermeneutical question is how to interpret what Scripture says—its insights into God and human existence that are contained in ancient thought forms and views of reality—into insights that are intelligible today, that is, into insights that reflect contemporary thought forms and views of reality. This is crucial if the Bible is to speak to us today and not simply show us what some ancient people thought.

The following example illustrates the problem. The earliest Christians, including that great apostle and missionary, Paul, lived with the lively expectation of the end of the world and the imminent return of Christ as judge of the living and the dead. This was the worldview they shared; it was part of the way they understood Christ and God's plan for human salvation. This understanding of reality meant that they did not have to worry about things like keeping Jesus' memory alive for long or about setting up institutions that would endure for centuries to promote the values that Jesus stood for. This worldview is not shared by many Christians today, and in fact when the end of the world, the end time, did not occur, the early Christian communities had to re-express their faith about Jesus. They did not simply lose their faith because the end time did not arrive. Instead, they restated their beliefs in ways that did not reflect this expectation of an imminent end. They did so by thinking about a distant, not imminent, end of the world.

Today, Christian communities must continue this task. The worldview of ancients is not binding on Christians today, especially when it contradicts our experiences of reality so much. Thus, as another example, when Paul recommends that people remain unmarried, like himself, because the end of the world is nigh and that they ought to prepare themselves for it, we today are not bound to follow his recommendation, which, emerging from his expectation of the end of the world, is inappropriate for us today. The same can be said for the role of women in the Christian community and the dominance of male God language in the biblical texts, two issues very much alive today, which can illustrate the issue of the interpretation of Scripture. Scripture reflects the dominant patriarchal attitudes and structures of the communities in which it emerged and was used. This is part of the very human dimension of Scripture and should be expected, not wondered at. You can see this the next time you read through the Old Testament. Notice how often it is important for a woman to bear a son. Sons were important because carrying on the family name was important, and the family name was carried on *through the male*, not the female. Females, when they married, left their own family and became part of their husband's family.

But we are moving into ways of thinking and interacting in which such patriarchal attitudes that support the domination of men over women are increasingly unacceptable. Our culture is responding to the demands by many women for equal treatment when it comes to participation in society and to employment. Our culture is recognizing that in the roles men and women play, and in how they interact, justice and mutuality, not domination, are the important values.

An important question emerges: how much weight ought we give to contemporary experience, values, and attitudes, especially in terms of judging the experience, values, and attitudes of Scripture? It might be easy to see that this critique is essential when it comes to our scientific understanding of reality; we simply cannot hold to prescientific worldviews concerning the development of the universe and retain any form of intellectual integrity. But when it comes to values and attitudes, the matter becomes much more problematic. The case of male-female relations is a case in point. Why should our sense of the injustice of patriarchal attitudes make us critical of such attitudes in the Bible?

This task of identifying valuable aspects of contemporary experience and engaging in the critique of Scripture, as well as translating the time-bound views of ancient times into the present, occurs in the Christian community. In reading Scripture and reflecting upon it in light of contemporary experience, the Christian community attempts to discern fundamental values and attitudes that it recognizes as "true."

Some of the cultural values and attitudes will stand out as criticizing Scripture, and Scripture will at times judge negatively some of the contemporary cultural values and attitudes. Which value criticizes which? That is the key problem. What this requires can only be self-authenticating. As the discerning community reflects, certain values and attitudes will stand out and strike a responsive chord in the hearts and minds of those in the community. To return to our example, the contemporary sensitivity toward the equal dignity of men and women has struck most Christians as a true attitude to have, and so this is critical of any scriptural passage that promotes the opposite perspective.

Some of these fundamental values and attitudes may be critical of Scripture itself. The Old Testament prophets' call for justice, for example, may include a critique of the patriarchal attitudes of Scripture. Using Jesus of Nazareth as the ultimate model for human living is important in this. Certain contemporary expressions of insights about God and human existence that express the values and attitudes of Jesus of Nazareth will strike a responsive chord in the hearts and minds of the community. They will stand as authenticating themselves, and regarded as quite simply true.

This approach toward the interpretive, or hermeneutical, question and the ongoing authority of Scripture is best undergirded by an understanding that the Divine is in some way present to created reality and to human beings. Certain expressions of how best to understand God and human existence will thus strike humans as true because they are intuitively recognized as appropriately or adequately expressing what is "felt" in the very depths of their being. Christianity has expressed this idea in its conviction that the church, the Christian community, is led by God's Spirit; it is influenced and moved by God's ongoing presence. In the Catholic Tradition, the Second Vatican Council of the mid-1960s talks about reading the "signs of the times." The Spirit of God is at work in the world, even beyond the boundaries of the church, and is calling the church to take note of movements and values outside of it.

This chapter has maintained that the best way to understand Scripture is to see it as the human Word of God. In and through the human words of Scripture, the Christian communities experience the reality of God and God's address to humankind. The geology professor mentioned at the beginning of this chapter is right when he says that the Bible presents us with an ancient and outmoded understanding of the development of the universe. But we can see why. How could the biblical author or authors know anything about the evolutionary process that has generated the universe? One of the great tasks of Christians is to interpret this time-bound, historically conditioned address of God in contemporary ways. This is a task that we will attempt to do in the second part of this book. It is a task that is carried out and continues in the church's Tradition. It is to this topic that we must turn now.

QUESTIONS FOR REFLECTION AND DISCUSSION
1. Think about what came to your mind when you heard the word "Bible" before you read this chapter. Has your view changed? Explain.

2. Other religious traditions (for instance, Islam, Hinduism, Buddhism) have "scriptures." Find out what you can about the scriptures of at least two other religious traditions. What is your attitude toward them? What would you say about their status in relation to the Bible? Why?

3. This chapter has argued that the Bible is the human Word of God. Does this approach make any sense to you? Are you better able to understand the Bible? What is your reaction? Explain.

4. How do you understand the Bible as "inerrant"? Do you agree or disagree with the argument of this chapter? Elaborate. What do you think about the statement that the Bible is inspired? What has this chapter said? Do you agree or disagree? Why?

Suggested Readings

Barr, James. *Escaping From Fundamentalism*. London: SCM, 1984.

Brown, Raymond E. *The Critical Meaning of the Bible*. Mahwah, N.J.: Paulist Press, 1981.

Hopper, Jeffrey. *Understanding Modern Theology, I: Cultural Revolutions and New Worlds*. Philadelphia: Fortress Press, 1986.

Hill, Brennan, R., Paul Knitter, and William Madges. *Faith, Religion & Theology: A Contemporary Introduction*. Mystic, Conn.: Twenty-Third Publications, 1992. See especially chapter 10.

CHAPTER FIVE

TRADITION

*S*ola Scriptura! "Scripture alone is the basis for all Christian thought and practice!" This was one of the defining rallying cries of the great Reformers of the sixteenth century, men like Martin Luther and John Calvin. "Scripture and unwritten traditions handed down by the church are the basis for Christian thought and practice." This was the reply of Catholics in that turbulent century. And the two sides fought each other at times to the death over these two stances. The issue of Scripture and Tradition has been a contentious one in Protestant-Catholic relations since then, and it still is for some. A few years ago at a family gathering, the reaction of an uncle upon discovering that his nephew taught theology was, "Is your theology biblically based?" He was really asking if the theology was based on the Bible alone.

The Reformers were concerned with what they called human traditions that could not be found in the Bible, traditions that were being made mandatory for Christian belief and practice. They looked at such things as compulsory fasting, priestly celibacy, and the selling of indulgences, and when they read the Bible they could not find Christ commanding or mentioning any of these. Human traditions might be legitimate, but to be mandatory for Christians something had to have a biblical basis to it, the Reformers insisted. The Catholic side, for its part, was convinced that God was ever present in the church, particularly to the pope, directing the church in what the pope said. Could the church, then, be in error in what it taught? Of course not! The traditions that had emerged in the church that had no biblical basis nevertheless came from God who was ever present to the church, preserving it from error.

What is Tradition? Why is it important? Indeed, *is* it important? The Reformers saw Tradition as a purely human addition to God's absolute word in Scripture, and, as human, it could be fallible and sinful. The Catholic side looked upon Tradition as divinely inspired. In a sense, both sides had some of the truth, but in a way neither could imagine. To see this, we must have an idea of what Tradition is and how it functions in the Christian community, as contemporary theology, for the most part, sees it.

Meaning of Tradition

The best way to begin is to provide a working definition. Tradition is the way the Christian community responds to its foundational revelation in what it says and does, and, once a body of writing has been accepted as Scripture, the way it interprets that Scripture, down through the ages. One can say that Tradition is the ongoing, living response to and understanding of revelation. As such, it is a dynamic reality, more like a living organism that responds to an ever-changing environment than a static block of truths and practices that are passed intact from age to age.

The starting point is, once again, revelation. You will recall from the discussion of revelation in Chapter Three that revelation involves a profound experience of the Divine. As a result of this experience, people say things and they feel compelled to act in certain ways. For example, in the case of Christianity people experienced a God who loved them and a call to love others. They talked about this God and their experience of God. They celebrated their foundational revelatory experience in forms of ritual. In short, a whole host of ways of thinking and acting developed as a result of revelation. And this continues throughout the course of history. This is Tradition.

In Christianity, then, Tradition includes the doctrines, or teachings, of the Christian communities. These state what these communities believe to be valid ways of articulating their understanding of reality in light of revelation. Most people may be familiar with this in the form of certain creedal statements, such as the Apostles' Creed. Tradition also includes the way the Christian communities worship. Worship is a ritual response to the experience of the Divine; the experience is celebrated and its meaning for human existence is reflected on in the context of a worshiping community. The Catholic eucharistic liturgy, or a Sunday celebration of the Lord's Supper in some Protestant churches, is an example. Tradition includes the moral codes that the Christian communities advance as ways of responding to the Divine (or negatively, as ways inconsistent with a proper response to the Divine). In short, the total life of the Christian community, everything that it says and does as it responds to its foundational revelation, is its Tradition.

Some of this Tradition will be more important and more authoritative than others. And this has led to the useful distinction between Tradition and traditions. The first, Tradition, consists of teachings and practices that are central to Christianity's very essence. For example, Christians say that God has saved humankind from its sinful state through the life and person of Jesus of Nazareth. Jesus is our Savior! This affirmation (which we will investigate more thoroughly in Part Two of this book) expresses a central conviction of Christianity. To deny this would be to make of Christianity something very different. The major creeds of Christianity, such as the Apostles' Creed or the Nicene Creed are creedal expressions of Tradition. The other, traditions, refers to beliefs and practices which do not have to do with the very substance of Christianity. To change these would not result in such a radical change in Christian identity that Christianity would be something unrecognizably different. The obligation of celibacy for clergy is an example. Catholic Christianity allowed priests to marry up until the eleventh century. Eastern Christian churches have always allowed a married clergy. Protestant Christianity has, as well. Yet all these are legitimately Christian. This tradition can change and this would not affect what is of the essence of Christianity.

Tradition plays a very important role in the Christian communities. It is in and through their various traditions that the foundational revelatory experience on which Christianity is based becomes present and real for the members of these communities. This was so for the first generations of Christians. They had no Scripture as we know it. The memory of Jesus and why he was important was kept alive in the Tradition of the early church. From this Tradition, the writings that we call the New Testament emerged. It is also in and through these traditions that Christians live out the implications of that foundational experience in their present social and historical context.

What about Scripture and Tradition, that central Reformation concern? As pointed out already, Scripture, in fact, arose out of the Tradition of the early church. But once the Christian communities decided that a particular group of writings authentically interpreted or witnessed to their foundational experience of God, then these writings, Scripture, became normative. They have guided the communities in their ongoing response to revelation throughout the course of history. Scripture, it is important to note, does not provide all of the answers to questions that the Christian communities face down through the ages. New questions will emerge in different historical times. For example, Scripture does not say anything about nuclear warfare or genetic engineering. Yet Scripture can provide values and attitudes that will help the Christian communities decide how to answer questions about these issues. In this sense, Scripture is a guide and a norm for Tradition. The two are not separate and unrelated, but are very much connected to each other in a dynamic process as the Christian communities exist throughout time.

HUMAN DIMENSION OF TRADITION

Like Scripture, Tradition is profoundly human. The doctrines that have emerged in the history of Christianity, the moral precepts that the churches issue, the various liturgies and celebrations that are part of Tradition—all of these responses to revelation that comprise both Tradition and tradition—have come from human beings as they have attempted to respond appropriately to God's foundational breaking into human consciousness. And so, like Scripture, Tradition will reflect the historical and cultural situation of its human authors and their humanness in all its dimensions. The truths that Christianity teaches do not simply drop down from heaven directly from God. Rather, they have emerged and do emerge still as a result of an interplay between the Divine and the human beings caught up in the experience of the Divine.

This way of understanding Tradition constitutes a major part of the Copernican revolution in Christian thinking today, especially in Catholic thought where there has been a tendency to regard the major doctrines of Christianity in much the same way that fundamentalists regard the Bible. One can encounter this attitude repeatedly in college theology classes. Many evangelical Protestant students are horrified when there is talk about the Bible as a human document. Many Catholic students, willing to accept the human dimension of Scripture, become horrified when there is talk about the same holding true for the church's teachings, even its central teachings. The emphasis has been so much on the divine side of things that the human input, the human conditioning, has been minimized or not even thought of. Thus, in 1973 the Catholic church could say about its dogmatic statements (those teachings it regards as central to Christianity) that

> . . . even though the truths which the church intends to teach through her dogmatic formulas are distinct from the changeable conceptions of a given epoch and can be expressed without them, nevertheless it can sometimes happen that these truths may be enunciated by the sacred magisterium in terms that bear traces of such conceptions.[1]

Notice that this statement says that the dogmatic statements of the church *may* be formulated in terms of the particular conceptions of a given time, but *can be expressed without them*. This is impossible, in the understanding presented above. All the statements of any Christian community will inevitably reflect the historical, cultural milieu in which they emerge with the particular thought patterns and world-views of those who enunciate them. *All* of them, without exception.

Tradition, then, develops; it is not a static, once-and-for-all thing. It develops in different ways, but the most important way is in response to changes in the cultural perspectives and environment of the Christian communities. The example of the doctrine of creation will help to illustrate this. When the understanding of the universe as "evolving" over billions of years asserted itself as the dominant and best way of understanding the development of the universe, the way Christians understood God as creator and the world as created had to undergo a radical change from the time when the dominant view was that the world was created "as is" in six days. Christians have been forced to reinterpret and re-express what they mean by creation, unless, that is, they want to continue to hold to an outmoded world-view—and thereby make Christianity, literally, something that speaks of an alien world.

THE HERMENEUTICAL PROBLEM AGAIN

This brings up the problem of hermeneutics, or interpretation, once again. When it comes to Tradition, the problem is basically the same as that connected with Scripture: how to transfer and re-express the culturally conditioned ways God and the human situation are understood from one time and cultural framework into another. The problem arises because people really do understand and experience reality in very different ways at different times. The lenses through which people experience reality and talk about it differ from one culture to another, from one age to another.

Religious beliefs and practices must be reinterpreted. But how does this process of interpretation and re-expression work? This is one of the key theoretical questions that confront theologians today, and there is no easy explanation of what goes on. It is a process that requires a dialogical and imaginative encounter with the received Tradition, and it is usually sparked by the perception that "something seems funny" about this Tradition. The Tradition just seems to be inconsistent with our experience and understanding of reality. The words used or the view of reality presupposed strike us as "odd," of a different world. Or, what it emphasizes seems to miss other dimensions of the Tradition.

An overview of this hermeneutical process looks like this. The received Tradition strikes us as problematic and so we look at it. We try to understand it on its own terms as much as possible. What were the authors of a particular doctrine trying to say? How did they understand things? What did their words and ideas mean to them, in their social-cultural setting? Then we bring our own questions and values and worldview into the picture, which both critiques the past tradition but is also critiqued by it. In this process we can discern values, attitudes, dispositions, or insights that strike us as important, as speaking to us, and that in some way resonate or strike a responsive chord. The final step is the act of interpretation in which we formulate an understanding of reality in light of our encounter with the past tradition. We are struck by a particular insight or value and then struggle to express it in terms of our own cultural horizon. This understanding will not be exactly the same and so this is an imaginative act in which an *analogous* attitude or disposition or value or insight is evoked.

Let's look at the Christian doctrine of creation as an example and return to June, the astronomer in Chapter One. She is interested in this Christian doctrine that the world was created by God. As she looks at the way Christians have understood the creation of the world in the past, she sees immediately that the past tradition is based largely on a reading of the opening chapters of the book of Genesis in the Bible as historical fact. According to this traditional doctrine, God created the world and everything in it in six successive days and rested on the seventh day. She discovers that enterprising scholars even calculated the date of the beginning of the world at 4004 B.C.E. Her reaction is one of bemusement. "How odd; how antiquated." She thinks in terms of billions of years! But then she is struck by some of the affirmations of this story. The ancient story tells of God as the origin of all things, willfully creating a world. Unconsciously, but imaginatively, she sees the story calling on her to think about her understanding of the development of the universe. She comes to see that the Big Bang is not an arbitrary, meaningless event, that reality is more than a churning cosmic sea generating randomly and without purpose all the things that so amaze her as she looks through her telescope. "All of this has a reality we call God as its source. There is meaning and purpose to it." These are the insights that captivate June as she considers creation. But note: her understanding of the doctrine of creation is one not based on an historical reading of the biblical story. It is an understanding shaped by her understanding of the cosmos and the forces at work in it. It captures insights that the old story and the old doctrinal expression evoke in her imagination.

Re-expressions of the Tradition do not convey *exactly* the same thing as was conveyed before, yet they can continue this Tradition in a way that can legitimately be called continuous with the past expressions. They can evoke similar attitudes toward God, for example. They can advance similar values or evoke analogous experiences of the Divine. They themselves will be culturally and historically conditioned, and they will thus never be able to articulate "the Truth" in an absolute way. Yet, they can be experienced as "true" and as "continuous" with the past because of a kind of "discernment," a kind of connaturality, in which the Christian community "feels" that the expression concerned captures something of the truth about God and human existence in relation to God that the older formulation expressed.

As suggested in the previous chapter, Christians can ground the legitimacy of this "intuitive" approach toward the development of the Christian Tradition and its reinterpretation on their conviction that God is present to the Christian community. This ongoing presence of the Divine allows for some expressions to be "felt" as truly legitimate re-expressions of the original revelatory experience and others as incompatible or as inadequate. This does not mean to say that an accepted re-expression will be absolutely adequate or the final word. These re-expressions are always profoundly human ones and inevitably culturally conditioned. As humans experience reality differently, as they come to newer understandings of their world, there will always be the need for ongoing reinterpretations of the Tradition so that it will more adequately express the "truth" about God, reality, and the human condition. In the second part of this book we will deal with a number of the major Christian teachings and will attempt to re-express them in a way that is both continuous with the insights of the past and makes sense to our times (at least to our particular culture).

In the opening paragraphs of this chapter, we discussed the old Reformation debate over Scripture and Tradition. In a sense, the Reformers had something of the truth about Tradition—it was human. Yet they would not have included the great Christian creeds (the Apostles' Creed and the Nicene Creed) as human. They would have regarded them as logical deductions from the Bible, which was absolutely true and from God, and so were quite different from traditions such as mandatory fasting. What this chapter has insisted on, as well as the previous one, on Scripture, is that in all cases, whether we are talking about Scripture or Tradition or tradition, we are talking about phenomena that are thoroughly, completely *human*. This approach to understanding these things distinguishes current Christian thinking from that of Christian thinking in the past.

The Catholic side talked about a divine source for its Tradition. When it comes to understanding Tradition, Christians must take this seriously, as well. In and through its various traditions, Christians are responding to that foundational revelatory presence of God, mediating it to the present. Moreover, Christians also are convinced that God is present to them, to individuals and to their communities, and this presence grounds their sense of appropriateness for new expressions of their Tradition. Tradition is, in a very real sense, *divine*, too.

NOTE

1. *In Defense of the Catholic Doctrine on the Church: The Declaration Mysterium Ecclesiae of the Sacred Congregation for the Doctrine of the Faith* (June 24, 1973), *The Pope Speaks* 18 (1973): 155.

QUESTIONS FOR REFLECTION AND DISCUSSION

1. What comes to mind when you hear the word "tradition"? Is your immediate reaction a positive one or a negative one? Express your reasons why.

2. Think of what you would call the tradition of your culture or a social group to which you belong. How does this tradition function?

3. Our access to the Divine occurs in and through the Tradition of the church. Explain. Can you give examples of the Tradition of your religious community?

4. Tradition, like Scripture, is profoundly human. What does this mean? Does this make any sense to you? Explain. What implications do you see in this for the teachings of the church?

SUGGESTED READINGS

Hill, Brennan R., Paul Knitter, and William Madges. *Faith, Religion & Theology: A Contemporary Introduction.* Mystic, Conn.: Twenty-Third Publications, 1992. See especially chapter 11.

Hodgson, Peter C., and Robert H. King, editors. *Christian Theology: An Introduction to Its Traditions and Tasks.* Revised edition. Philadelphia: Fortress, 1985. See especially chapter 2.

O'Collins, Gerald. *The Case Against Dogma.* N.Y.: Paulist Press, 1975.

O'Collins, Gerald. *Fundamental Theology.* Mahwah, N.J.: Paulist Press, 1981. See especially chapters 7, 8.

CHAPTER SIX

RELIGION AND RELIGIONS

S tanding at her office window, which overlooks the quadrangle on the university campus, a theology professor gazes at the great variety of students and staff passing below, people from different cultural backgrounds and different countries. As one who is professionally interested in religion and theology, she is struck by the variety of religions that they represent. There are Sikhs, with the men wearing their distinguishable turbans. Muslim women pass by, wearing the traditional *purdah*. A Jewish friend from the Zoology Department goes by. She knows that some of the people she sees are Christian. Others are Hindus. There are even a small number of Buddhists. In short, there is a notable religious diversity here, men and women from different religions who daily pass her office. And this situation is not unique. Many cities and towns in North America and in Europe experience the same phenomena. We live in increasingly religiously pluralistic societies.

Have you ever thought about the religions of other people? If not, what do you think of when you read of this woman's experience? Are other religions truly "from God" in the sense that a real experience of the Divine stands at their base? What about the behavior and the values they promote? Are these in any sense "good"? Is your attitude positive or negative toward other religions and their followers? Do you think Christianity is superior to these other religions? Or are all religions equally acceptable? And why are there so many different religions? These are the sorts of questions that Christians have asked and continue to ask today as they experience men and women of differing religions living and working in their midst.

Meaning of Religion

We begin our discussion of these questions by talking about religion itself. How we might understand what religion is has been the subject of some debate in Christian thinking. In general, there have been two approaches that represent the way Christians have understood and continue to understand the term "religion." One general approach has been to say that religion is the human attempt to know God and attain salvation. The emphasis here is on the human. This view of religion sees people as being concerned with the ultimate questions about life and seeking the Absolute, God, and also seeking salvation from the distortions of human existence. The religions that have emerged throughout the world are manifestations of this quest. Christians who adopt this understanding of religion, though, place Christianity on a different level than other religions. They say Christianity is based on God's revelation. What Christianity says about God and salvation comes from God, the result of God's breaking into human history to reveal the divine Self and to offer salvation. In Christianity we encounter more than the human attempt to know God and attain salvation.

The second general approach is to see the religions of the world as the various culturally conditioned ways in which human beings have responded to God's revelatory activity. God, in this view, has entered human consciousness in particular times and places, and human beings have responded in different ways to this divine inbreaking. Religion and revelation thus go together. Religion is not simply human. It is indeed human, but it is the human response *to God*, to revelation. This response includes the sacred writings of a religious tradition, that religion's teachings, its moral codes, the way it celebrates its foundational encounter with the Transcendent, even its organizational structure. In this approach, Christianity is not inherently different from the other major religions of the world.

Relationships Among the Religions

The two ways of understanding "religion" have resulted in a number of ways that Christians have understood the relationship among the religions of the world. It is possible to categorize these as an exclusivist approach and an inclusivist approach, each with two subsections.

The first, the *exclusivist approach (a)*, sees religion and revelation as "hostile" to each other. They are hostile because religion is the *human* attempt to attain what God alone can give, namely, knowledge and understanding of the Divine and of salvation. Religion is the futile, indeed prideful, human effort to grasp at that which God alone can grant. God's revelation, which in the Christ event supremely breaks into human history, shows the folly and futility of this effort.

This exclusivist approach sees God's revelatory activity as confined to the Judaeo-Christian tradition. God has entered human history in a revelatory way *only* in the events of the formation of the people of Israel and ultimately and decisively in and through the life of Jesus of Nazareth, who is the Word of God addressed to human beings. God has entered history in the events witnessed to in the Bible that formed the basis of Judaism, then, but these have been completed and surpassed in God's revelation in the Christ event. God's revelatory activity is found only in these events, nowhere else. Christianity, based as it is on God's ultimate revelatory activity, is the only "true" religion and is thus superior to other religions.[1]

A slightly different manifestation of this tendency to see God's revelatory activity as concentrated exclusively in the Judaeo-Christian tradition is *exclusivist approach (b)*. Exclusivist approach (a) tends to see religion and revelation as opposing each other. Exclusivist approach (b) tends to see revelation as completing or perfecting the human attempt to know God and attain salvation. This approach dominated Catholic thinking during the first half of this century and is still in evidence in official Catholic statements on the world's religions. Humans, in their efforts to understand God, find these aspirations fulfilled when God comes in self-revelation. Humans are offered the way to salvation when God comes in revelation. The non-Christian religions, as manifestations of the human quest for God and salvation, are called *natural religions*; Christianity is called *revealed religion*. This approach (b), like the first one outlined above (a), upholds the inherent superiority of Christianity in relation to other religions. You can get a sense of this in a 1985 address of Pope John Paul II:

In religion man seeks answers to the [fundamental questions of life] and in different ways establishes his own relationship with the "mystery which engulfs our being." Now the various non-

Christian religions are above all the expression of this quest on man's part, while the Christian faith is based on Revelation on God's part. And here—notwithstanding some similarities with other religions—lies the essential difference with regard to them.[2]

The second general approach to understanding the religions of the world, the *inclusivist* approach, insists that religion and revelation go together. The various religions of the world emerge as a result of humankind's response to God's inbreaking. Like the exclusivist approach, this second approach has two major Christian manifestations.

Inclusivist approach (a) sees all the religions, especially the world's major religions, as human responses to revelation, yes, but Christianity is that religion that is based upon God's definitive, highest revelation. It is in and through the Christ event that God, in a definitive, unsurpassable way, breaks into human consciousness to reveal the divine Self and to offer humans salvation. The inherent superiority of Christianity is maintained, yet this approach acknowledges that other religions are not merely human but are responses to God's real revelatory activity as well.

Inclusivist approach (b), sometimes called the pluralistic approach, sees the *major* religions of the world as all equally valid responses to God's revelatory activity. Such activity is different in different cultures, and the human response differs according to the particular culture concerned, but we cannot say that any one culturally conditioned human response is better than others. There are many revelations and many human ways of responding to revelation, all valid. Christianity is thus not inherently superior to Islam or Judaism, or Hinduism, for example. One favorite illustration of this approach is that of a group of blind persons touching various parts of an elephant and describing what they experience. All of the descriptions, of course, are different. All of the blind persons are describing an experience of the elephant, but each has a partial experience and describes the experience from his or her unique perspective. This analogy is applied to the various major religions of the world in their response to God's revelatory presence.

INTERRELIGIOUS RELATIONS

What should the attitude of Christians be toward the women and men of other religions and toward these religions themselves? The most appropriate attitude includes commitment and openness, that is, commitment to one's own religion, Christianity, as that religion in which God has revealed Self and in which God offers salvation, and openness to other religions as providing the means by which other persons also meet God and are offered salvation. This means accepting one of the inclusivist approaches discussed above. There are a number of reasons for adopting this approach rather than the exclusivist approach. One of the strongest is based upon the essential social nature of human beings. We live and flourish not as individuals alone but as members of communities. We are inherently social beings. It seems quite logical to suppose, then, that God meets us in and through the institutions that are integral aspects of any community. God addresses us not only individually, but in and through the social structures that we create.

Indeed, the experience of Christians is just this. The church, the Christian community, is the primary place for the encounter with God. It is in and through the community and its structures, chiefly through the reading of the Word of God in Scripture and in the ritual celebration of our foundational experiences of God, that God is encountered and made present. It seems reasonable to say, then, that the religions of the world are institutional structures through which the Divine is made present to people. We might suppose that God meets us only in and through Christianity, but that would mean that others do not encounter God. What is more, if the encounter with God has a saving dimension to it, then these others would not have access to salvation. This is quite simply an abhorrent view of God and is inconsistent with the Christian understanding of God as a God of love who wills that all be saved.

Added to this is an experiential argument. When we actually encounter men and women of other religious faiths, we encounter persons who can only be described as truly holy persons, touched by the presence of God, leading upright, decent lives. Moreover, it seems to be that they are like this not despite their religious tradition, but because of it. Their religion fosters and encourages their attitudes and values. Christianity has no monopoly on persons who are devout, holy, and morally upright. This existential contact with outstanding, decent human beings who are not Christian can and should lead to the conclusion that these people, too, have been touched by God, and further, that their religious traditions have had a positive role in this.

This respect for other religions and their followers need not diminish the respect for and the commitment to one's own religious tradition. Humans are finite and are historically and culturally situated. We cannot believe all things at once. Our encounter with the Divine is, moreover, a particular culturally grounded and mediated encounter. We can be committed to this fully, even as we respect the commitment of others. It may be that God has addressed human beings in an unsurpassable and definitive way in and through Jesus of Nazareth. This ought not lead Christians to disparage other religions such that their value in mediating God's presence and healing power is diminished or negated. Genuine respect is a legitimate attitude to have toward other religions. Such an attitude need not threaten one's Christian commitment at all.

Nor need it prevent one from speaking proudly of one's faith and the experience of the Divine that grounds it. The experience of God and the view of reality that results naturally impel one to share the truths that are perceived. This sharing, however, is best done in dialogue, which involves sharing what one has and listening respectfully to the dialogue partner. Dialogue does not deny proclamation of one's faith or witness to it. Indeed, dialogue can include proclamation and witness. Yet it also demands a willingness to listen and hear what the other says. A dialogical approach to the faith convictions of others, then, is an approach that *invites* others to listen to what one has to say. It does not demand that they be converted.

NOTES

1. This is the view of the influential Protestant theologian, Karl Barth. See, for example, "Karl Barth: The Revelation of God as the Abolition of Religion," in *Christianity and Other Religions: Selected Readings,* edited by John Hick and Brian Hebblethwaite (Philadelphia: Fortress, 1981), pp. 32-51.
2. "Relations With Non-Christian Religions." Address of John Paul II, June 5, 1985. From *L'Osservatore Romano* (Eng.), June 10, 1985, p. 9.

QUESTIONS FOR REFLECTION AND DISCUSSION

1. List all the religions you are aware of. What do you know about each of them?

2. What is your attitude towards non-Christian religious traditions? Why do you have this attitude?

3. If you adopted the pluralistic approach outlined in this chapter, what effect would that have on your understanding of Christianity? Do you think that this would be a bad or a good thing? Elaborate.

4. Think about your attitude towards non-Christian religions (ques-

tion 2). What implications does this attitude have when it comes to relating to their followers?

SUGGESTED READINGS

Hick, John. *God Has Many Names.* Philadelphia: Westminster, 1982.

Hick, John, and Brian Hebblethwaite, editors. *Christianity and Other Religions: Selected Readings,* Philadelphia: Fortress, 1981.

Hill, Brennan R., Paul Knitter, and William Madges. *Faith, Religion & Theology: A Contemporary Introduction.* Mystic, Conn.: Twenty-Third Publications, 1992. See especially chapters 6-8.

Knitter, Paul. *No Other Name? A Critical Survey of Christian Attitudes Toward World Religions.* Maryknoll, N.Y.: Orbis Books, 1985.

McBrien, Richard P. *Catholicism.* 2nd ed. San Francisco: HarperCollins, 1994. See especially chapter 10.

Sullivan, Francis A. *Salvation Outside the Church? Tracing the History of the Catholic Response.* Mahwah, N.J.: Paulist Press, 1992.

CHAPTER SEVEN

OUR LANGUAGE ABOUT GOD

The prayer most often recited in Christian Tradition begins, "Our Father, who are in heaven . . ." Christians refer to God as Father, Son, and Holy Spirit. In the worship of most Christian communities, God is "he." Why is this? Is God male, so that male language is most appropriate for speaking of God? We are living in the midst of a significant shift in cultural perspective that has begun to question this type of language about God. The feminist movement, as it is called, has challenged the exclusive identification of godliness with masculinity. And this challenge is meeting much opposition. "The Bible, after all, calls God 'he.'" "Jesus himself called God 'Father.'" "How can we change what the Bible so clearly says?"

The question about male language used of God touches upon a wider issue, the very language we use generally to talk about God. It also touches upon the nature and authority of Scripture and Tradition. In this final chapter of Part One, let us look at these issues surrounding our language about God.

Our language about God has always been "strange" language. The reason for this lies in the fact that such language is always about a reality that we experience as *unlike* any other we know. It speaks about an Ultimate, Transcendent, and "totally other" reality. We are forced to use language derived from our experiences of this world to speak about what is "other" than these or "more" than these. Such language, then, always fails to grasp completely the nature or reality of what it refers to; it is always off the mark in some way. And herein lies the great problem when it comes to religious language: such language is *never literal, but always analogous.*

This problem has led to the emergence of what is called the *via negativa*, the "negative way" of talking about God. In this way, one says what God is *not*. For example, God is infinite (not finite), or God is immortal (not mortal). This type of language certainly conveys the experience of "otherness" that is part of our experience of the Divine. But is it all that we can say? Is there not some "positive" content that can be conveyed in our language about God? Christian Tradition has replied affirmatively to this. While admitting the legitimacy of the *via negativa*, it has also insisted that we can say something positive about God which in some way captures the reality of God. This is possible, however, only if there is an "analogy of being." That is, the "being of God," or God's reality, cannot be totally like us and created reality, which is obvious, or totally unlike us, either. Claiming that positive God-language is possible only if there is some "analogy of being," does not, however, *prove* that the Divine is, in some way, like created reality. The existence of some sort of likeness, however, is the *felt experience* of Christian Tradition, just as is the experience of the otherness of the Divine.

ANALOGY

A useful way of describing our language about God is to say that it is analogical language. An analogy is a statement that at the same time both affirms and denies something about something else. If we say that God is our father, in analogical language we are saying in effect that God is like a parent to us; at the same time, we are affirming that God is unlike any parents we know. There is, in other words, a yes-no quality to this kind of language. To use another example: God is a shepherd and we are the flock of God's pasture. Experience of the Divine has introduced this shepherd-sheep image into our religious tradition as an appropriate way of talking about God and ourselves. We do not mean, however, that God is literally a shepherd or that we are literally sheep. We are saying that God possesses, in a preeminent way, those qualities we associate with a shepherd's relationship to his sheep and that it is appropriate to describe God and our relationship to God in these terms. These terms capture something of the reality of the Divine and our relationship to the Divine.

While such language might be "appropriate," it is never completely adequate or exact. What is more, as indicated in the chapters on Scripture and on Tradition, such language does not magically drop down from heaven. It emerges from us, or better, it emerges from the reflections and experience of the religious community as it struggles to express an understanding of the Divine. Both of these things must be considered in any proper reflection on the sort of language we use about God: its inadequacy and its profoundly human origin.

SYMBOL

Yet another way of understanding religious language is through the notion of "symbol." A symbol is something that makes something else present to us. In the discussion of revelation, it was noted that in a revelatory experience there is some medium, some event, person, or thing that triggers an awareness of the Divine. This medium, or symbol, makes the Divine present to our consciousness. The language that results from this encounter can also be regarded as symbolic; these words mediate to us the reality of God. What is crucial to note about symbols is their power to bring us into contact with some aspect of the reality they symbolize. Yet, although symbols can do this, they are also other than what they symbolize; they are not literally and completely what they mediate to us. They thus conceal as well as disclose. Religious language, as symbolic, is like this: it both discloses and conceals the reality of God. And so, it is both adequate and inadequate at the same time.

SEXUALLY INCLUSIVE LANGUAGE

When we speak of the predominance of male language when Christians talk about God, the concern is not that such male language is inappropriate or wrong. The concern, rather, is that when it becomes exclusive it becomes too much of a distortion about God. Why is this? Why is the exclusive use of male language to talk about God too restrictive and counterproductive? Simply put, it fails to take seriously enough the inadequacy of all language about God; it also tends to exclude other language that would serve to enlarge or enrich our understanding of God. God may indeed appropriately be thought of as a "father," but God cannot be restricted to this image. God is more; God transcends all the images we may use. An exclusive use of male images distorts our understanding of God in the sense that it raises one set of finite images up to a level with the Divine as if these were the only ways of talking about God. Maleness becomes identified with God, as if maleness belongs to the essence of God, while femaleness does not.

Why has male language dominated the Christian Tradition's language about God? It has because of the dominant position of men in the cultures in which such God-language developed, and not because male language is the most appropriate way to speak about God. In other words, the human dimension of our traditional language about God is the reason for this phenomenon. Such language is culturally conditioned, reflecting the worldview of particular cultures. We should not be surprised, then, that our language about God is so male dominated. We have to understand that our language about God can never really grasp the reality of God, or ever exhaust what can be said about God. This, plus the realization of the human dimension of all language about the Divine, has led Christians to begin rethinking the way they speak about God. Exclusive or dominant use of male terms is misleading and fails to express the richness of God. Other language, including female language, is needed so that Christians can more adequately arrive at an understanding of the Divine. For example, speaking about God as mother might draw our attention to a God who *gives life* and who nourishes and cares for life, better than speaking about God as father. And certainly, those things are "true" about God insofar as Christians have experienced God.

There is more to this movement away from the dominant use of male God-language. Language reflects a worldview, to be sure, and so the exclusive or dominant use of male God-language can be seen as reflecting a patriarchal worldview in which men are the ultimate paradigm for the human and have effective power. From a patriarchal perspective, it is "appropriate" that God be male since the male has preeminence. Language, though, also *promotes* a worldview, not just reflects it. Exclusive or dominant use of male God-language promotes the view that the ultimate, highest, preeminent reality is male and thus the female's position is diminished or denigrated. In other words, such exclusive or dominant God-language supports and reinforces a patriarchal structure in which men dominate and are determinative of what is human at the highest level. The Christian community must decide whether this worldview is consistent with its experience of God and especially whether it is consistent with the values and attitudes of Jesus of Nazareth who, it claims, is the highest manifestation of God.

As we shall see in Part Two when we look at the figure of Jesus and his life and activity, the reign of God that Jesus preached and promoted was a reign that overturned the usual power structures of his day. It was a reign of radical inclusion and communion where the separation between friends and enemies, those who dominate and those dominated, is overcome, and master-slave types of relationships are done away with. The movement to widen the Christian community's language about the Divine has, it would seem, a solid grounding in Christian Tradition because it is faithful to essential values and attitudes present in Christianity.

In this question of God-language, the chief point to keep in mind is the profound human dimension to such language and its profound inadequacy. This applies even to the biblical language about God. The essential question is not, then, exactly what does the Bible name God. It is: what are the central values and attitudes of Christianity, and does the language we use of God promote or negate these.

QUESTIONS FOR REFLECTION AND DISCUSSION

1. What words come to mind when you think of God? Make a list. Where have these words come from? Are you aware of other ways of talking about God from another religious tradition? If not, look up some of these.

2. Would you feel uncomfortable if God were called "she"? Explain your reaction.

3. What do you think of the assertion in this chapter that our God-language both reflects and promotes a particular worldview?

4. What do you think of changing or adding to the language the Bible uses about God?

SUGGESTED READINGS

Coll, Regina A. *Christianity and Feminism in Conversation*. Mystic, Conn.: Twenty-Third Publications, 1994. See especially chapters 1, 2.

Haight, Roger. *Dynamics of Theology*. Mahwah, N.J.: Paulist Press, 1990. See especially chapters 7, 8.

Hick, John. *Philosophy of Religion*. 3rd edition. Englewood Cliffs, N.J.: Prentice-Hall, 1983. See especially chapter 6.

Johnson, Elizabeth A. *She Who Is: The Mystery of God in Feminist Theological Discourse*. New York: Crossroad, 1992.

McFague, Sallie. *Models of God: Theology for an Ecological, Nuclear Age*. Philadelphia: Fortress, 1987.

PART TWO

DOCTRINAL THEMES

INTRODUCTION

This part deals with a number of central Christian doctrines, or teach-ings (the word "doctrine" comes from the Latin *doctrina,* which means "teaching" or "instruction"), that have to do with the basic vision of reality that Christianity sets forth. This vision of reality, this way of understanding the world, has emerged as a result of those profound encounters with God that constitute revelation. Thus, what Christians say about reality is not the result of human reflection alone, Christians insist. This vision of reality results from the human experience of God and is thus shaped in a very real way by God. There is a divine dimen-sion to it.

That is not the whole story, however. As we have seen throughout this book, there is a profound *human* dimension to Christianity, and this certainly includes the doctrines Christianity sets forth. The teach-ings of the Christian faith, then, are the result of the human attempt to articulate a vision of reality in response to the experience of God's rev-elatory presence. These teachings will inevitably reflect the social-his-torical context of their human authors with their limits, greatness, and foibles.

The understanding and experience of reality that Christians have today is very different from that of their ancestors in the faith. Thus, the contemporary way of articulating a Christian vision of reality will be different. Indeed, it will have to be different if Christians are to explain the content of their faith in the clearest and most coherent language available. The Christian vision of reality—what it teaches about the world, God, and human existence—will have to be intelligible to contemporary experience or it will be, quite simply, meaningless and irrelevant.

The remaining chapters of this book will attempt to outline a Christian vision of reality that is intelligible to human beings today. It will focus on the Christian doctrines about creation, human sinfulness, and Jesus as Lord and savior. It will show that these teachings open up to us a view of reality that both corresponds to the reality we experience *and* allows us to understand this reality in a better way.

In the discussion of Jesus as Lord and savior, there will be an extensive discussion of what is called the "quest for the historical Jesus." All Christian doctrines must in some way be referred to Jesus of Nazareth since he occupies the central place in Christianity. Christians claim that in and through him God reveals the divine Self, offering humans salvation. Our understanding of Jesus, though, is changing dramatically from that of our ancestors in the faith. A Copernican revolution is occurring in the way Christians think about Jesus and interpret his life, and this revolution involves the so-called Jesus of history and his significance. Exactly what this means and how this has an impact on the traditional Christian claims about Jesus will become apparent as we proceed.

CHAPTER EIGHT

CREATION

The geology professor we met in Chapters One and Four, you may recall, finds Christianity so antiquated and unworthy of serious attention because the biblical account of creation, if taken literally, is incompatible with the findings in his science. Indeed, the vast majority of his colleagues in all the other sciences would agree that this incompatibility exists. What about you? Have you ever thought about this? Are you aware of the assertions of the so-called creationists who insist that the biblical account is right and that the scientific model is wrong, a mere hypothesis or theory? There are many Christians making these claims today. And their attitude is the same as the geology professor: either science or the Bible.

In order to examine these question and arrive at an understanding of what the doctrine of creation really means—this is the main topic of this chapter—it is crucial to know what the ancient biblical accounts of creation actually say. These accounts have so shaped the consciousness of Christians when it comes to understanding creation that any reflection on this Christian teaching must pay attention to them. Notice that we have to speak of biblical "accounts." There are two of them in the opening chapters of the Bible, each with a distinctive style and distinctive understanding of the creation of humans and their world.

FIRST CREATION STORY

The first creation story in the Bible occurs in Genesis 1:1–2:4. It is the story that involves a seven-day scheme: God creates a world and everything in it, including human beings, in six successive days and rests on the seventh. It reads as follows:

In the beginning when God created the heavens and the earth, the earth was a formless void and darkness covered the face of the deep, while a wind from God swept over the face of the waters. Then God said, "Let there be light"; and there was light. And God saw that the light was good; and God separated the light from the darkness. God called the light Day, and darkness he called Night. And there was evening and there was morning, the first day.

And God said, "Let there be a dome in the midst of the waters, and let it separate the waters from the waters." So God made the dome and separated the waters that were under the dome from the waters that were above the dome. And it was so. God called the dome Sky. And there was evening and there was morning, the second day.

And God said, "Let the waters under the sky be gathered together into one place, and let the dry land appear." And it was so. God called the dry land Earth, and the waters that were gathered together he called Seas. And God saw that it was good. Then God said, "Let the earth put forth vegetation: plants yielding seed, and fruit trees of every kind on earth that bear fruit with the seed in it." And it was so. The earth brought forth vegetation: plants yielding seed of every kind, and trees of every kind bearing fruit with the seed in it. And God saw that it was good. And there was evening and there was morning, the third day.

And God said, "Let there be lights in the dome of the sky to separate the day from the night; and let them be for signs and for seasons and for days and years, and let them be lights in the dome of the sky to give light upon the earth." And it was so. God made the two great lights—the greater light to rule the day and the lesser light to rule the night—and the stars. God set them in the dome of the sky to give light upon the earth, to rule over the day and over the night, and to separate the light from the darkness. And God saw that it was good. And there was evening and there was morning, the fourth day.

And God said, "Let the waters bring forth swarms of living creatures, and let birds fly above the earth across the dome of the sky." So God created the great sea monsters and every living creature that moves, of every kind, with which the waters swarm, and every winged bird of every kind. And God saw that it was good. God blessed them, saying, "Be fruitful and multiply and fill the waters in the seas, and let birds multiply on the earth." And there was evening and there was morning, the fifth day.

And God said, "Let the earth bring forth living creatures of every kind: cattle and creeping things and wild animals of the earth of every kind." And it was so. God made the wild animals of the earth of every kind, and the cattle of every kind, and everything that creeps upon the ground of every kind. And God saw that it was good.

Then God said, "Let us make humankind in our image, according to our likeness; and let them have dominion over the fish of the sea, and over the birds of the air, and over the cattle, and over all the wild animals of the earth, and over every creeping thing that creeps upon the earth."

So God created humankind in his image, in the image of God he created them; male and female he created them.

God blessed them, and God said to them, "Be fruitful and multiply, and fill the earth and subdue it; and have dominion over the fish of the sea and over the birds of the air and over every living thing that moves upon the earth." God said, "See, I have given you every plant yielding seed that is upon the face of all the earth, and every tree with seed in its fruit; you shall have them for food. And to every beast of the earth, and to every bird of the air, and to everything that creeps on the earth, everything that has the breath of life, I have given every green plant for food." And it was so. God saw everything that he had made, and indeed, it was very good. And there was evening and there was morning, the sixth day.

Thus the heavens and the earth were finished, and all their multitude. And on the seventh day God finished the work that he had done, and he rested on the seventh day from all the work that he had done. So God blessed the seventh day and hallowed it, because on it God rested from all the work that he had done in creation.

These are the generations of the heavens and the earth when they were created.

There are a few things to note about this story. First, it reflects a premodern view of the universe in which the "heavens" are a metal dome on which the stars and the sun and moon have been placed and around which they revolve. There are waters above these "heavens" and rain is caused by the opening of floodgates through which the waters pour down. God dwells above the waters over the heavens. The earth is flat. Here is an illustration of the world the way prehistorical people visualized it.[1]

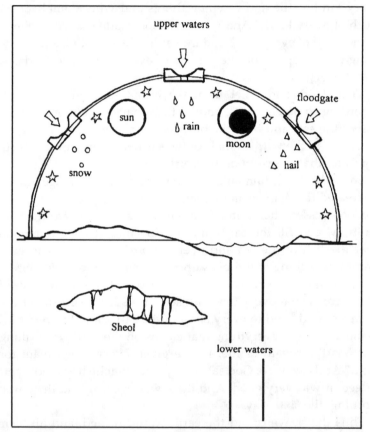

In the story, God is absolutely in charge of things; there is no rival power that stands against God. Everything in the universe comes from the one God's creative word and so everything else is created or is a creature. God alone is God! What is more, God's creation is essentially good, willed into existence by God. It is no mere accident that there is a world. Finally, human beings are the crown of God's creative energy. There is something special about them.

SECOND CREATION STORY

The second creation story follows immediately after the first, in Genesis 2:4–24. It involves the creation of "Adam and Eve" and their being placed in the garden of Eden. It is obviously a different story: the order of creation differs (note that a human being is created before the animals and the vegetation) and the way God creates differs. In this story, God "forms" things and in the case of the human being "breathes" life into the human one so that a living being is created. Even the name for God is different. In the first story, the word "God" is used while in the second story the words "Lord God" are used. This second story of creation reads as follows:

> In the day that the Lord God made the earth and the heavens, when no plant of the field was yet in the earth and no herb of the field had yet sprung up—for the Lord God had not caused it to rain upon the earth, and there was no one to till the ground; but a stream would rise from the earth, and water the whole face of the ground—then the Lord God formed man from the dust of the ground, and breathed into his nostrils the breath of life; and the man became a living being. And the Lord God planted a garden in Eden, in the east; and there he put the man whom he had formed out of the ground. The Lord God made to grow every tree that is pleasant to the sight and good for food, the tree of life also in the midst of the garden, and the tree of the knowledge of good and evil.
>
> A river flows out of Eden to water the garden, and from there it divides and becomes four branches. The name of the first is Pishon; it is the one that flows around the whole land of Havilah, where there is gold; and the gold of that land is good; bdellium and onyx stone are there. The name of the second river is Gihon; it is the one that flows around the whole land of Cush. The name of the third river is Tigris, which flows east of Assyria. And the fourth river is the Euphrates.
>
> The Lord God took the man and put him in the garden of Eden to till it and keep it. And the Lord God commanded the man, "You may freely eat of every tree of the garden; but of the tree of the knowledge of good and evil you shall not eat, for in the day that you eat of it you shall die."
>
> Then the Lord God said, "It is not good that the man should be alone; I will make him a helper as his partner." So out of the

ground the Lord God formed every animal of the field and every bird of the air, and brought them to the man to see what he would call them; and whatever the man called every living creature, that was its name. The man gave names to all cattle, and to the birds of the air, and to every animal of the field; but for the man there was not found a helper as his partner. So the Lord God caused a deep sleep to fall upon the man, and he slept; then he took one of his ribs and closed up its place with flesh. And the rib that the Lord God had taken from the man he made into a woman and brought her to the man. Then the man said,

"This at last is bone of my bones and flesh of my flesh; this one shall be called Woman for out of Man this one was taken."

Therefore a man leaves his father and his mother and clings to his wife, and they become one flesh. And the man and his wife were both naked, and were not ashamed.

Like the first story, God is in charge. All things depend on God for their very being. The world exists because God willed it. But there is more. God does everything for the well-being of the human creature God creates. God arranges for an idyllic garden in which the human creature is placed. Seeing that the human creature is alone, God creates first the animals and then the woman, a suitable partner for the man. God *cares* for the human creatures and puts them in charge of creation to look after things. The first human beings are not God's playthings or puppets. They have responsibilities and tasks and are given the freedom to think and act for themselves in carrying out their tasks. Finally, they do not have the ultimate say about things, despite their freedom and responsibilities. God commands them not to eat the fruit of the tree of the knowledge of good and evil. What they want is not the definitive measure of all things.

INSIGHTS IN THE CREATION ACCOUNTS

These two accounts of creation sound incredible to the ears of the geology professor mentioned earlier and of all who are engaged in mainstream scientific investigation. We have to admit that there is a real incompatibility between the sciences and the Bible if one sees these accounts as presenting a literal, historical description of the origins and development of the universe. There simply is no way to harmonize the two biblical accounts with the scientific model on this level. And the vast majority of theologians who work in academic circles recognize this incompatibility. Moreover, they accept the scientific model of evolution as best describing "what really happened" to produce our universe.

What do we do with the biblical accounts of creation, then? The first thing is to recognize that they reflect a prescientific understanding of reality and accept them that way. This ought not be surprising. In fact, it should be taken for granted. This is because, as stated in the discussion of Scripture, the Bible has been written by human beings and reflects their social-historical situation. Of course, then, the accounts of creation will reflect no awareness of an evolutionary understanding of the development of the universe. How could anyone living before the emergence of the modern sciences have had even the slightest awareness of what contemporary science tells us? Such a person lived very much in another world!

Once we accept that these stories reflect a prescientific worldview and thus are not descriptions of what took place, we must go on to deal with them at another level. Of course, we might regard them as interesting historical curiosities, revealing the mind-set of ancient peoples. Yet they need not simply be so regarded. As Scripture, they can still be influential in revealing to us important truths about God, ourselves, and the reality in which we live.

If these stories are to function in this way, though, we must engage in that process of hermeneutics, or interpretation, that we discussed in the chapter on Tradition when the astronomer, June, looked at these stories and allowed them to inform her imagination.

What might we come up with when we engage in this process of interpretation? Perhaps one of the most important truths the creation stories tell us is that neither the world nor human beings are the ultimate reality and measure of all things: God is. In both stories, God is ultimately responsible for all of created reality. As important as human beings are, they are creatures, dependent on God for their very being. And so, they are not the most important or most fundamental of all the realities in the universe. This priority of God is further emphasized in the second creation story by God's command not to eat the fruit. Humans do not have unlimited, absolute freedom to do anything they want; they are not to set the criterion for all else. God, rather, is the ultimate point of reference to whose will humans are called to bend their wills. This point is very important to keep in mind because one of the dominant worldviews prevalent today is secular humanism which does indeed hold that humans are the ultimate measure of all things. The Christian vision of life says "no" to this. God's will is ultimate;

humans are called to seek and enact God's will and not place their own above God's.

Now lest this make human existence appear servile and demeaned, we must note that an important affirmation of Christianity is that God's will and human well-being go together. Indeed, it is not too much to say that God's will *is* human well-being. Nowhere in the creation stories is there any suggestion that God creates just for pleasure or to make servile puppets. The second story brings this out well. Everything that God does is for the benefit of the human person God has created. God makes a garden for this first human and places this human over it. God creates a suitable partner for this first human. Even when the pair of humans rebel and are forced out of the garden, God makes clothes for them, the story says. God is concerned for the welfare of the humans created.

This concern of God for human well-being cannot be overemphasized. God, that ultimate reality upon whom all things depend, *cares* for created reality and for the humans created. God is not a distant, aloof, indifferent First Cause, or a hostile power over and against humans. God is, rather, *for* humans, on their side, desirous of their well-being. This is a most significant insight that emerges from these ancient creation stories.

There is, moreover, an essential goodness to created reality. The first creation story brings this out clearly in its repetition of God's viewing creation as "good." This aspect of that first story is important because of the long history, in the Christian tradition, that tended to downplay matter, even regarding it as evil, compared to the good "soul." We humans are not in a situation in which there is evil matter and good spirit. We may abuse matter and use it for our purposes, but it is not essentially evil.

It is the same for human sexuality. There has been a long distrust and denigration of human sexuality in the Christian tradition. Like the denigration of matter, this comes from the mistrust and even denial of the goodness of the material and the bodily that characterizes much of the Greek philosophy prevalent in the first few centuries of the Christian movement. But in the first creation story, God blesses the fruitfulness of the humans.

For our present era, the biblical stories of creation have something to say about how we deal with our environment. Environmental concerns are very important, today because we are realizing more and more just how much we have abused our environment and how this abuse is causing serious and even deadly problems for us. In the second story of creation, the earth creature is told to look after the garden. Caring for this garden is a sacred trust, certainly incompatible with exploiting and destroying it. It is not too much of a leap to say that this second creation story invites us to care for the world in which we have emerged. We are not here to diminish it or harm it. Moreover, this created reality, this environment in which we live, is good. Humans are invited to keep it that way, not abuse it as something evil.

What is more, the first creation story has God creating humans in the divine image. What this means for the biblical author is explained like this: "Then God said, 'Let us make humankind in our image, according to our likeness; and let them have dominion over fish of the sea, over the birds of the air, and over the cattle, and over the wild animals of the earth, and over every creeping thing that creeps upon the earth.'" As the notes of the New Revised Standard Version of the Bible say, the idea of being created in God's image refers to relationship and activity. Humans are commissioned to be like God in their relationship with everything else. And how does God exercise care in this story? God creates an environment in which things *flourish* and which is essentially good!

A final aspect of the creation stories worth noting is that humans are called to live in community, not as isolated individuals or set in opposition to others. In the first creation story, God creates humans in a pair, male and female. There is no solitary, lonely person. A human community is created right from the start. In the second creation story, God sees that the first human is lonely, that it is not good for this person to be alone, and so goes about providing a suitable partner, the woman. Persons living together in community is the way God wills things in these stories.

The old stories of creation need not simply be historical relics of a bygone time; they continue to speak to us today. They can be the occasions for promoting a worldview that includes the features noted above. As for the doctrine of creation itself, it tells us: 1) that humans are *creatures*, not gods; 2) that human life is geared toward recognizing and carrying out God's will, which is essentially our well-being; 3) that we are called to be stewards of an essentially good creation; and 4) that we live as members of community. This doctrine does not necessarily involve teaching how the world or the universe or human life came to be the way they are. That is the domain of the natural sciences. Yet the real importance of this doctrine remains: it tells us about ourselves, our situation, our relationship to God, one another, and the world.

Note
1. The diagram is adapted from Larry Boadt, *Reading the Old Testament: An Introduction* (Mahwah, N.J.: Paulist, 1984), p. 115.

Questions for Reflection and Discussion
1. What is your position regarding the creationist vs. scientific accounts of the origins of the universe? Why do you hold the position you do?

2. Explain the approach this chapter takes toward the biblical stories of creation. What is your reaction? Explain.

3. What is hermeneutics? Why does this chapter insist that a process of hermeneutics must be applied to the biblical accounts of creation?

4. Has this chapter added anything to your understanding of the Christian teaching about creation? If so, elaborate. If not, explain.

Suggested Readings

Fiorenza, Francis Schüssler, and John P. Galvin, editors. *Systematic Theology: Roman Catholic Perspectives*. Volume 1. Minneapolis: Fortress, 1991. See chapter 4.

Hayes, Zachary. *What Are They Saying About Creation?* Mahwah, N.J.: Paulist Press, 1980.

Hodgson, Peter C., and Robert H. King, editors. *Christian Theology: An Introduction to Its Traditions and Tasks*. Revised edition. Philadelphia: Fortress, 1985. See especially chapter 5.

Trible, Phyllis. *God and the Rhetoric of Sexuality*. Philadelphia: Fortress, 1978. See especially chapter 4.

CHAPTER NINE

THE DOCTRINE OF SIN: THE HUMAN PREDICAMENT

The author of the first creation story in the Bible presents a story in which God, after creating the world and all animals, pronounces them good. What is more, after creating human beings, God says that they are very good. There is an essential goodness to created reality. But that cannot be the whole story. Indeed, it does not take long for any of us born into this world to experience all kinds of deception and depravity. A mere glance at the newspaper or watching the newscast confirms this. Our world is beset by murders, war, acts of terrorism, sexual abuse, and injustice. We are threatened by the pollution that results from exploiting the earth in our industrial, technological culture. At times, our lives seem to be meaningless. Human existence, we think, is not as it should be. Something is wrong. There is profound distortion. You could list many examples from your own experience.

The Christian tradition has attributed much, if not all, of the dysfunction of human existence to what it calls "sin." The doctrine of Original Sin in particular has been very influential in the way Christians have understood the human predicament. First elaborated in a systematic way by Augustine, bishop of the northern African city of Hippo in the fifth century, this doctrine shaped the way Christians up until our present century have understood their reality. Although this doctrine is problematic for many today, it is so much part of the Christian heritage that some re-expression of it is necessary.

The doctrine of Original Sin has at its basis the biblical story of the Fall of the first humans. This story completes the second creation story we looked at in the previous chapter. The biblical author and the tradition behind that author's story was well aware that this was not the "best possible world." Something was amiss. The story of the Fall was an attempt to come to grips with this experience of a world that was not as it ought to be.

BIBLICAL STORY OF THE FALL

Because of the deep and widespread influence this story has had in shaping the Christian consciousness in terms of understanding the human plight, it is important to know its details. It reads as follows:

Now the serpent was more crafty than any other wild animal that the Lord God had made. He said to the woman, "Did God say, 'You shall not eat from any tree in the garden'?" The woman said to the serpent, "We may eat of the fruit of the trees in the garden; but God said, 'You shall not eat of the fruit of the tree that is in the middle of the garden, nor shall you touch it, or you shall die'." But the serpent said to the woman, "You will not die; for God knows that when you eat of it your eyes will be opened, and you will be like God, knowing good and evil." So when the woman saw that the tree was good for food, and that it was a delight to the eyes, and that the tree was to be desired to make one wise, she took of its fruit and ate; and she also gave some to her husband, who was with her, and he ate. Then the eyes of both were opened, and they knew that they were naked; and they sewed fig leaves together and made loincloths for themselves.

They heard the sound of the Lord God walking in the garden at the time of the evening breeze, and the man and his wife hid themselves from the presence of the Lord God among the trees of the garden. But the Lord God called to the man, and said to him, "Where are you?" He said, "I heard the sound of you in the garden, and I was afraid, because I was naked; and I hid myself." He said, "Who told you that you were naked? Have you eaten from the tree of which I commanded you not to eat?" The man said, "The woman whom you gave to be with me, she gave me fruit from the tree, and I ate." Then the Lord God said to the woman,

"What is this that you have done?" The woman said, "The serpent tricked me, and I ate." The Lord God said to the serpent, "Because you have done this,

> cursed are you among all animals
> and among all wild creatures;

upon your belly you shall go,

> and dust you shall eat
> all the days of your life.

I will put enmity between you and the woman,

> and between your offspring and hers;

he will strike your head,

> and you will strike his heel."

To the woman he said,

> "I will greatly increase your pangs in childbearing;
> in pain you shall bring forth children,

yet your desire shall be for your husband,

> and he shall rule over you."

And to the man he said,

> "Because you have listened to the voice of your wife,
> and have eaten of the tree

about which I commanded you,

> 'You shall not eat of it,'

cursed is the ground because of you;

> in toil you shall eat of it all the days of your life;

thorns and thistles it shall bring forth for you;

> and you shall eat the plants of the field.

By the sweat of your face

> you shall eat bread
> until you return to the ground,
> for out of it you were taken;
> you are dust,
> and to dust you shall return."

The man named his wife Eve, because she was the mother of all living. And the Lord God made garments of skins for the man and for his wife, and clothed them.

Then the Lord God said, "See, the man has become like one of us, knowing good and evil; and now, he might reach out his hand and take also from the tree of life, and eat, and live forever"— therefore the Lord God sent him forth from the garden of Eden, to till the ground from which he was taken. He drove out the

man; and at the east of the garden of Eden he placed the cheru-
bim, and a sword flaming and turning to guard the way to the
tree of life (Genesis 3:1–24).

The following points are important in understanding the story.
First, the sin of the first humans is that of wanting to rival God. The
temptation of the serpent is really: "You will be like God." There is an
act of disobedience, to be sure, yet the real sin is their attempt to
replace God by setting themselves up as gods, too. The pair forget their
status as creatures. As the story unfolds, the results are disastrous.
Because they have "sinned," that is, because they have tried to set
themselves up as gods, replacing the real God, the harmony that used
to be present now disappears. They realize that they are naked and are
ashamed. The man dominates the woman: something is amiss
between them. They try to hide from God: the positive relationship
between themselves and God has crumbled. They are even alienated
from the natural environment: only by hard, difficult work will it be
possible to make a living. In short, all sorts of negative consequences
issue forth from this terrible offense. The final event in this story of the
Fall is that God drives the two out of the garden and they no longer
have access to the tree of life, a tree whose fruit provided immortality
for them. Suffering and death are now features of human existence.
Yet, God still cares. God provides them with clothes before they leave
the garden. God has not repudiated the pair completely.

DOCTRINE OF ORIGINAL SIN

A literal reading of the story of the Fall undergirds the way that
Christian tradition developed the doctrine of Original Sin. Remarks of
that great early Christian missionary, Paul, also influenced the shape
of the doctrine. In his letter to the Christian community at Rome in the
60s C.E., Paul contrasts Jesus, the "new Adam," to the old Adam. He
writes in Romans 5:12–21:

> Therefore, just as sin came into the world through one man, and
> death came through sin, and so death spread to all because all
> have sinned—sin was indeed in the world before the law, but sin
> is not reckoned when there is no law. Yet death exercised domin-
> ion from Adam to Moses, even over those whose sins were not
> like the transgression of Adam, who is a type of the one who was
> to come.

But the free gift is not like the trespass. For if the many died through the one man's trespass, much more surely have the grace of God and the free gift in the grace of the one man, Jesus Christ, abounded for the many. And the free gift is not like the effect of the one man's sin. For the judgment following one trespass brought condemnation, but the free gift following many trespasses brings justification. If, because of the one man's trespass, death exercised dominion through that one, much more surely will those who receive the abundance of grace and the free gift of righteousness exercise dominion in life through the one man, Jesus Christ.

Therefore just as one man's trespass led to condemnation for all, so one man's act of righteousness leads to justification and life for all. For just as by the one man's disobedience the many were made sinners, so by the one man's obedience the many will be made righteous. But law came in, with the result that trespass multiplied; but where sin increased, grace abounded all the more, so that, just as sin exercised dominion in death, so grace might also exercise dominion through justification leading to eternal life through Jesus Christ our Lord.

The key point to note is Paul's idea that through Adam's sin, sin and death have entered the world and that, furthermore, *all* are caught up in it. Sin has totally infected the whole human race. One might note the male-centered world of Paul, who does not mention Eve at all in his remarks.

While there were some differences in the way theologians explained the features of the doctrine, there were common features that emerged continually, at least in Catholic articulations. They are:

1. *The state of perfection before the Fall.* The first human pair lived in an idyllic garden and enjoyed the blessings of God. In most Catholic articulations of this from the Middle Ages down to the middle of this century, this meant that they lived in a state of sanctifying grace, that is, they shared in God's life inasmuch as creatures could. They also enjoyed what were called the preternatural (more than what was natural to them) gifts of freedom from suffering and death. What is more, their minds and wills operated as perfectly as possible for humans. In short, their existence was as perfect as creaturely possible, and even more so, for they were given more than they could naturally have, namely, sanctifying grace and the preternatural gifts.

2. *The Fall.* Tempted to rival God, the pair sinned. The sin of disobedience was prominent in most traditional discussions. They were not forced to disobey, however. The doctrine insisted that their sin was something they freely committed. Sin cannot be blamed on God. A misuse of human freedom lies at the root of the human predicament.

3. *The consequences of the sin.* As a result of their sin, God punished them. They lost their sharing in God's type of life, that is, they lost sanctifying grace (according to the Catholic understanding of the event). They also lost the preternatural gifts of freedom from suffering and death. Furthermore, they were alienated from God. They had lost the divine favor and a gulf now existed between themselves and God.

4. *Further consequences of the sin.* Other dreadful consequences followed, as well. Significantly, the minds of the pair were now "clouded"; now, they could only with great difficulty use their reasoning and thinking powers to arrive at truth. Their wills were "weakened"; now they preferred evil to good. Indeed, in some articulations of this doctrine, they could no longer will to do good at all. They were filled with concupiscence, that is, their passions were no longer easily ruled, if at all, by their reason. In short, the pair were now "slaves to sin."

5. *The fallen state is passed on.* This state of fallenness, or brokenness, and alienation from God did not simply affect the first pair of humans. It was passed on to their descendants, and to theirs, and so on. Thus, every human being came into the world alienated from God and so was a sinner, and every human being existed in a fallen, broken condition. One of the great Protestant professions of faith, the Augsburg Confession, described this condition very starkly in the following way:

> It is also taught among us that since the fall of Adam all [people] who are born according to the course of nature are conceived and born in sin. That is, all . . . are full of evil lust and inclinations from their mothers' wombs and are unable by nature to have true fear of God and true faith in God. Moreover, this inborn sickness and hereditary sin is truly sin and condemns to the eternal wrath of God all those who are not born again through Baptism and the Holy Spirit.[1]

Protestant and Roman Catholic theology and piety differed with respect to the consequences of the Fall with the Protestant tradition tending to a more negative view of humanity after the Fall. But the important idea to bear in mind is that for both traditions humans were born into a fallen world, into a state of sin, without their having made any choices at all. What is more, so hopelessly caught in this situation were they that they could not, by their own efforts, remedy the situation. If there were to be any remedy, it would have to come from God.

DIFFICULTIES WITH THE STORY OF THE FALL AND THE DOCTRINE OF ORIGINAL SIN

During the last two centuries, but especially in the last fifty years, the traditional elaboration of the doctrine of Original Sin and the story of the Fall have become somewhat perplexing for many Christians. The story of the Fall as it stands literally is inconsistent with our contemporary understanding of the development of the human species, and it certainly strikes us as filled with what can only be called mythical elements. Talking serpents and a tree whose fruit provides immortality are mythical to us today, reflecting a world that is completely foreign to the world we experience. Talk of a perfect human pair, not beset by suffering, disease, or death, is not compatible with our knowledge of human development and the human condition. Once again, it reflects a world that is incredible. For these reasons, the vast majority of Christian biblical scholars today, as well as theologians, are convinced that the story of the Fall is not historically true.

This raises a number of questions with respect to the traditional way of understanding the human predicament in terms of that story and, indeed, in terms of the doctrine of Original Sin. What does one do with that ancient story? And what does one do with the doctrine of Original Sin, which was elaborated on the assumption that the story was historically true? It may be that both are irrelevant for us today. But that need not be. A revised understanding and re-expression of both are possible, for both have valuable insights for us if we are truly to understand the human predicament.

TOWARD A NEW UNDERSTANDING OF THE FALL

The story of the Fall cannot be accepted as an historical description of a pair of original humans. Yet there are insights into human existence that are worth our consideration as we reflect on the human situation. The following are a number of suggestions that the Christian tradition can seriously propose based upon a reading of this story.

The essential nature of the "sin" is the first point worth considering. "You shall be like God," the serpent says. The temptation is to rival God, to set up gods other than the true God. And the pair fall, wanting to set themselves up as gods. This story is really the story of the human race, the story of ourselves. We, and humans before us, are always tempted to replace God by something or someone else. We are tempted to commit idolatry, in other words, in various forms. And we fall, as have those who have preceded us. We attempt to center existence on ourselves and our will, making ourselves "number one." Or we try to center existence on other things, for example, on money, possessions, or our sexual appetite. We do this as individuals and also as communities. In various ways *we* are those first human beings insofar as we attempt to set up rivals to the one, true God.

As in the biblical story, the results of our idolatrous activities lead to disaster; they can also lead to enslavement or despair. For example, making ourselves the center of existence results in the attempt to subjugate others, individually and collectively, to what we want. Alienation and hostility result. History is filled with attempts of one nation or people to impose its will on others and the conflict this causes. Or, by way of another example, our search for money, possessions, or power leads to all the evils of greed. What is more, our continuing search for them is never truly satisfied. The more we get, the more we want. This is the common human experience. Driven to seek fulfillment in finite realities, our unfulfilled yearnings have two results. On the one hand, we become enslaved by the idols we seek, because in trying to find true fulfillment we end up pursuing them more and more, still hoping to find satisfaction. On the other hand, we can give up the search in despair. All the idols we set up fail to satisfy our infinite yearning. This attempt to replace God with idols results in disaster for ourselves and our world. This is the truth that emerges in the story of the Fall. There are grounds for it in our experience of life. "Adam and Eve" and what happened to them depict ourselves, the human race, and its story.

The story also indicates something essential to the Christian experience of the Divine, that God is the one who truly fulfills human existence, not the false gods that we constantly strive after. Living in right relationship to God (obeying God's command, in the story) leads to human fulfillment, and when humans turn away from God to rivals, they bring disaster upon themselves.

A NEW LOOK AT ORIGINAL SIN

We must abandon the traditional elaboration of the doctrine of Original Sin, as it stands, and reformulate some of its insights. The reason for this is that Christian Tradition based its doctrine on a literal reading of the Genesis story of the Fall. This is no longer tenable for the reasons given above. Yet the old doctrine does have a number of themes which, when re-expressed, disclose important insights about our existence: 1) we are born into a sinful situation, or environment, that we inherit from our predecessors, and (2) we are a broken people who pass on our brokenness to those who come after us.

We inherit a broken, sinful situation from our ancestors and suffer because of it, through no fault of our own. The old doctrine of Original Sin understood it as the sinful condition into which we were born *as a result of the sin of the first humans*. It does not take too much experience of the world to recognize that we are indeed "born into sin"; we are born into a world in which there is brokenness, alienation, harm done. This situation, of course, is not the result only of the wrongdoing of an original pair of human beings. Down through human history, human beings have made decisions that have harmed the well-being of others, and these decisions have become expressed in the very fabric of our various social structures. So, when we are born, we enter a world in which rivalry, hostility, and injustice abound. The black baby born into the apartheid system of South African racism suffered, through no fault of his or her own, from this situation, a situation that resulted in the impoverishment and diminishment of the well-being of millions of blacks. Palestinian and Jewish babies are born into a situation of hatred and conflict. We do not enter a morally neutral or good world and proceed to make it better or worse by our own decisions. We enter into a world that is, to use the traditional Christian expression, "fallen," and sinful. The world is sinful because these situations that cause harm are not accidental; they are the result of human decisions.

The traditional doctrine of Original Sin has more to teach us. It reminds us of our brokenness, both as individuals and as communities. The old doctrine, in its Catholic presentation, talked about our "wounded nature," with our minds clouded and our wills weakened. The Protestant tradition referred to a "corrupted" nature. In these views, we were not innocents born into the world, but were inherently broken people. It might be better to say, today, not that we are born *as* sinners but that we *become* sinners or broken persons as we grow up in our culture and undergo the processes of socialization of that culture. This requires further elaboration.

When we are born into a particular society and grow up in it, we are "educated" in various ways and adopt particular attitudes and values about ourselves, our relationship with others, and with God and our world. All of the social structures and institutions of our society promote particular ways of understanding ourselves and our world. For example, if we are born into a society dominated by a capitalist, market-driven economic system, we may be "told" in all sorts of ways that the world "is" a marketplace and we must compete against others. Life is presented to us as a competitive struggle to "get ahead." Our society might teach us that whites are better than Native Americans or Chinese or blacks. In short, as we grow up, we adopt as our own the values and attitudes of our society unconsciously. They become part of us, part of the way we understand reality. We adopt these attitudes in all of their brokenness, and that is the most important thing to reflect upon in this discussion. We become broken people, we become "infected" with sin, our minds become "clouded," as it were. The doctrine of Original Sin can remind us of this. It can alert us to the (inevitable?) presence of values and attitudes that have become part of our very being which cause harm to other persons and ourselves.

There is one more point to make. The doctrine of Original Sin presupposes an awareness—better, a belief—that our existence is not as it should be, that attitudes and actions that cause harm are distortions that create a distorted world. These are not "natural," inevitable, the way things have to be. The old story of the Fall with its picture of a perfect world reflects this faith perception on the part of the biblical author, as does the doctrine of Original Sin on the part of the Christian community. Moreover, the story and the doctrine reflect the faith perception that a truly fulfilled human existence is an existence lived in positive relationship to God and to other humans. It is this that we are called to make real in our lives.

NOTE
1. *The Augsburg Confession*, Anniversary Edition (From *The Book of Concord.* Translated and edited by Theodore G. Tappert, Fortress, 1959) (Philadelphia: Fortress, 1980), p. 10.

QUESTIONS FOR REFLECTION AND DISCUSSION
1. Reflect upon your life. What experiences do you consider negative experiences? Which ones are positive? Why?

2. This chapter has argued that the biblical story of the Fall is not an

historical story. Why? What do you think of this? Is the story useful for your understanding of the human situation? Explain.

3. Have you heard of Original Sin before reading this chapter? If so, describe how you understood it. What does this chapter say about Original Sin? Does it make any sense to you? Explain.

4. How do you understand what *sin* is? Has this chapter added anything to your understanding? Elaborate.

SUGGESTED READINGS

Hayes, Zachary. *What Are They Saying About Creation?* Mahwah, N.J.: Paulist Press, 1980. See especially chapter 5.

Hellwig, Monika K. *Understanding Catholicism*, chapter 3. Ramsey, N.J.: Paulist, 1981.

Hodgson, Peter C., and Robert H. King, editors. *Christian Theology: An Introduction to Its Traditions and Tasks.* Revised edition. Philadelphia: Fortress, 1985. See especially chapter 7.

McBrien, Richard P. *Catholicism*, chapter 5. New edition. San Francisco: HarperCollins, 1994.

CHAPTER TEN

JESUS OF NAZARETH: THE CONTEMPORARY PROBLEM

We exist in a fallen world, as fallen creatures. This is what Christian Tradition has said in its doctrine of Original Sin. But that is not the end of the story. Christian Tradition has also said that God, out of love, has saved us from this predicament. In particular, God has saved us in and through Jesus the Christ. Jesus is our savior!

Who is this man, Jesus of Nazareth? What has he done? How is he related to God? What do you think of when you hear the name of Jesus? A gentle man, "meek and mild," sporting a halo? God walking upon the earth? At Christmas time, you may think of a small baby in a manger, surrounded by animals and angels. At Easter, the image of a man bursting out of a tomb may come to mind. Or do you think of a man nailed to a cross, suffering in agony before dying? Perhaps you may picture a man healing a leper. Most of us have images like these when we think of Jesus. We also have different understandings of his importance.

Christian theology deals with the question of Jesus under the general themes of the *person* of Jesus and the *work* of Jesus. The first category has the technical name of "Christology" (from the Greek words *christos*, Christ, and *logos*, reason or talk; hence, reasoning about the Christ); the second is called "soteriology" (from the Greek words *soter*, savior and *logos*; hence, reasoning about the savior). In each of these areas, there has truly been a Copernican revolution in the theology of our time. The understanding of who Jesus was, what he did, how he was (is) related to God, and how he can be our savior is very different today from that of previous generations of Christians. Indeed, in this area of Christian reflection, Christian communities are struggling to articulate adequate new expressions of their beliefs.

COPERNICAN REVOLUTION IN CHRISTOLOGY

It is useful at the beginning of this study of the person and work of Jesus to be aware of the major shifts that have taken place in Christological reflection, at least in a general way. This revolution in Christology has two major, but related, features. The first is the recognition of and insistence upon the genuine and complete humanity of Jesus. Christians have from the earliest days associated Jesus with God and even came to call him divine. Indeed, so much emphasis has been placed on the divinity of Jesus that the other aspect of Jesus, his humanity, has been at times denied, downplayed, or not seriously considered at all. It was Jesus' divinity that has most often been the controlling and influential aspect of his person and work. Yet Christian Tradition has also always insisted on the human aspect of the person of Jesus. This is what is now front and center. If anything, it is his divinity that is troublesome, the subject of much reflection and debate. Reflection on Jesus has been stood on its head, so to speak.

The second feature of contemporary Christology is a shift from what is called a "Christology from above" (or a "descending Christology," or a "high Christology") to what is called a "Christology from below" (or an "ascending Christology," or a "low Christology"). The so-called classical Christology, that is, the kind of thinking about Jesus that took place from the time of the formulation of the classic doctrines about Jesus in the fourth and fifth centuries, was a Christology "from above." It began its reflection on Jesus from the divine side of things. Jesus was the Word of God, the second person of the Trinity, come down from heaven, taking on our humanity in order to save us. The prologue to the Gospel of John exemplifies the basic structure of this approach.

In the beginning was the Word, and the Word was with God, and the Word was God. He was in the beginning with God. All things came into being through him, and without him not one thing came into being. . . . And the Word became flesh and lived among us. . . . (1:1–3, 14)

The "Christology from below," on the other hand, begins its reflection on Jesus by focusing on his humanity and what as a real human being he said and did. The human Jesus is thus its starting point. Then it goes on to reflect upon Christian Tradition's claim that Jesus was and is also divine. The two approaches are exactly the opposite in their starting points. We will reflect on the two Christologies again in Chapter Fourteen.

When the Christology from below takes the humanity of Jesus seriously, it is important to be aware of just how serious this is. Jesus was a real human being with all the limits and the conditioning that are necessarily part of human existence. This means that he was an historically conditioned being just as all humans are. Jesus had to grow in his understanding of his surroundings and struggle against limits, ignorance, and sin just like everyone else. He was not some alien figure inserted into our world free from the limitations and the conditions we all face. So, he reflected a particular time and place; he thought and acted like a first-century C.E. Palestinian Jew and not, for example, like a Greek born in that century.

One of the important aspects of the Christology from below, and the recognition of the real humanity of Jesus that characterizes most contemporary theological reflection on Jesus, is the search for the "historical" Jesus. This is the Jesus that can be recovered, or discovered, by using historical methods. The question of the historical Jesus has been a thorny one for the past hundred years. It involves a number of questions, two of which are: Why is finding the Jesus of history a problem, anyway? and, Why is the historical Jesus so important? In the remaining pages of this chapter we will deal with these two questions and introduce the contemporary search for the Jesus of history.

PROBLEM OF THE GOSPELS

For many Christians, the issue of the historical Jesus is a strange one. What is the problem, anyway? After all, don't we simply have to open up the Bible, turn to the four gospels, and there find the Jesus of history? Well, the matter is not quite that simple. Yes, the Jesus of history is there, but below the surface. The presentation of Jesus that is found in the gospels is more a presentation of what is called the "Christ of faith." To understand this, we must look at the gospels and the problems they pose.

The gospels are virtually our only sources for information about Jesus. There are other sources that refer to Jesus, but they tell us very little about his life and deeds. In the New Testament, outside of the gospels, we encounter very little other than general summaries of what Jesus said and did. For example, in the Acts of the Apostles (2:22–23) we read about Peter who, after the experience of the Holy Spirit at Pentecost, proclaims to the crowds:

> You that are Israelites, listen to what I have to say: Jesus of Nazareth, a man attested to you by God with deeds of power, wonders, and signs that God did through him among you, as you yourselves know—this man, handed over to you according to the definite plan and foreknowledge of God, you crucified and killed by the hands of those outside the law.

There is very little information about the details of Jesus' life here and no quotation of words.

Non-Christian sources are of little help in advancing our knowledge. There are few references to Jesus that can be regarded as truly authentic and all that one can glean from them is that Jesus lived, that he was put to death by Pontius Pilate, the Roman ruler in Palestine, and that a movement sprang up after him. Thus, the Roman writer Tacitus, commenting on the Roman Emperor Nero's attempt to blame Christians for a devastating conflagration in Rome, remarks:

> . . . Nero created scapegoats and subjected to the most refined tortures those whom the common people called "Christians," [a group] hated for their abominable crimes. Their name comes from Christ, who, during the reign of Tiberius, had been executed by the procurator Pontius Pilate.[1]

We must turn to the gospels, those four accounts that on the surface present us with a "life story" of Jesus, to find out more about him.

We must take care when we do this, however. The gospels are not eyewitness accounts of Jesus' life. They do not present us with a factual, impartial record of his life and teaching. This is because they are documents, written by believers, designed to encourage and promote particular views of who Jesus was and what he did. They are writings, moreover, written on the basis of sources that were far from ideal in piecing together a life story of this man. The best way to come to an understanding of this and its implications for our knowledge about Jesus is to outline how the gospels came to take the shape they have.

Development of the Gospels

Mainstream contemporary biblical scholarship says that the gospels as we now have them developed out of a process that had three stages. The first stage centers on the origin of the material that found its way into the gospels. This origin was, of course, the life and teaching of Jesus of Nazareth, who had a profound effect on a number of people while he was alive. His life was ended when he was put to death by crucifixion. But that was not the end of him. Some time after his death, certain of his followers claimed that they had experiences of him as alive, as having been raised from the dead. They began to proclaim him as, among other things, the Messiah of God who would soon return at the end of the world and judge the living and the dead. A missionary movement began in which this message was preached, and communities of people who came to be called "Christians" sprang up around the Mediterranean Sea in the Roman Empire. The second stage in the formation of the gospels was under way.

This second stage in the formation of the gospels can be called the stage of developing traditions about Jesus, a stage that went on for some thirty years or so before the first gospel was written, and indeed continued for some time after that. The general contours of this stage seem to have included the following. In the course of the preaching about Jesus, preachers would use illustrations of what they remembered or were told about the deeds and sayings of Jesus when he was alive. Hence remembrances of what he said about love of enemies, of what he said about who our neighbor was, and so forth, would illustrate this early preaching. Remembrances of things Jesus did, such as his healing of lepers and his eating with sinners, would exemplify the preaching as well. It is natural that embellishments and additions would be added, so that when Jesus' marvelous cures were recounted the astounding details would be enhanced. Often enough, the original context of a saying was lost, because it was not important for the purposes of illustration. Purely legendary stories of Jesus circulated. What is more, Jesus, hailed as the Messiah, was presented as fulfilling what people then thought of with respect to the coming of the Messiah.

Jesus' life was recounted and retold to make it consistent with this messianic expectation. Thus, stories circulated about Jesus, some of his sayings were retold, his deeds were recounted, additions and embellishments occurred, legendary tales arose, and what can best be described as a certain amount of "construction" and inventiveness took place as people remembered and reflected upon their Lord.

There was as yet nothing like a "life story" of Jesus. There was no felt need for this, since the earliest Christians appear by and large to have expected the return of Jesus in a second coming, the Parousia, and the end of the world fairly soon. But sometime in the late 60s or the early 70s C.E., someone called Mark wrote a unique and significant "life story" of Jesus that came to be called a "gospel." Later, someone who was given the name Matthew wrote a gospel, perhaps around the year 80 C.E. He probably knew Mark's gospel, and he seems to have used both it and a collection of material about Jesus (which biblical scholars call the "Q" source) as sources in writing his gospel. A little later, someone we call Luke did the same (around 85 C.E.), using Mark's gospel and "Q" as sources, too. Finally, sometime between 90 and 100 C.E., the gospel of John appeared.

The gospel writers, called evangelists, completed the process by which the gospels were formed. The third stage in the formation of the gospels was the actual writing of the gospels. The gospel writers used whatever material they had at their disposal and put together a story of Jesus as best they could. Most biblical scholars do not think any of the gospel writers were eyewitnesses to the life of Jesus, and thus they had to rely on the stories and the traditions about him that they had at their disposal. They did more, however, than simply gather together stories about Jesus and put them in some sort of order.

They were not interested only in factually recording Jesus' life. They were persons of faith who wanted to promote faith in Jesus. And they each had their own view of what was important about Jesus. Thus they fashioned the material about him and presented a particular view of Jesus, one that most likely responded to questions, concerns, and even controversies that their respective communities faced. They were redactors, or editors, giving their story of Jesus a particular focus or slant. Mark, for example, seems to address the problem of suffering and its meaning, for he emphasizes more than any of the other gospel writers the need of the disciples of Christ steadfastly to endure suffering, following the footsteps of the suffering Jesus. Matthew seems to address the question of how the church, the community of believers, relates to Judaism, because he, more than any other gospel writer, emphasizes that Jesus fulfills the expectations of Judaism concerning the Messiah. In short, each of the gospel writers advances a particular view of Jesus and addresses particular concerns. The gospels are not, then, simple life stories, of Jesus.

The story of Jesus' entry into Jerusalem immediately before his crucifixion, set up in parallel columns with the gospels of Mark, Matthew, and Luke, will serve to illustrate the shaping and constructive work of the evangelists as they wrote their story of Jesus. As you compare the three versions of the same event on page 95, note the differences you notice.

If one keys on Matthew's gospel and compares it to the other two, one difference is that there are *two* animals involved in his story. The disciples are told to bring a donkey *and* a colt, and Jesus rides on *them*. Mark and Luke refer to only one animal. What Matthew has done is apparent when one reads the prophetic verses he quotes. He refers to the book of the prophet Zechariah (9:9) which says:

> Rejoice greatly, O daughter Zion!
> Shout aloud, O daughter Jerusalem!
> Lo, your king comes to you;
> triumphant and victorious is he,
> humble and riding on a donkey,
> on a colt, the foal of a donkey.

In Matthew's view, Jesus is the Messiah who fulfills exactly the Jewish Scriptures. He thus changes the story he has received so that Jesus rides, incredibly, on two animals, thereby fulfilling the Scriptures to the letter! A form of "construction" has taken place so that a particular perspective, a particular understanding of Jesus, is put forward.

So much, in fact, has the gospel presentation of Jesus resulted from decades of a developing, circulating tradition about him and from the redactional activity of the gospel writers, who were all trying to advance the deeper *truth* about Jesus, that what one sees in the gospels is the faith conviction of the early church about him and the concerns and controversies of the early church. In other words, one sees in the gospels what has been termed the "Christ of faith." This is the figure the early Christian communities "constructed" and believed in. We are not presented with the bare "facts" of Jesus, but rather, and more importantly, with who he "really" was, that is, the underlying mean-

Mark 11:1–10	Matthew 21:1–9	Luke 19:29–38
1When they were approaching Jerusalem, at Bethphage, near the Mount of Olives, he sent two of his disciples 2and said to them, "Go into the village ahead of you, and immediately as you enter it, you will find tied there a colt that has never been ridden; untie it and bring it. 3If anyone says to you 'Why are you doing this?' just say this, 'The Lord needs it and will send it back here immediately'." 4They went away and found a colt tied near a door, outside in the street. As they were untying it, 5some of the bystanders said to them, "What are you doing, untying the colt?" 6They told them what Jesus had said; and they allowed them to take it. 7Then they brought the colt to Jesus and threw their cloaks on it; and he sat on it. 8Many people spread their cloaks on the road, and others spread leafy branches they had cut in the fields. 9Then those who went ahead and those who followed were shouting, "Hosanna! Blessed is the one who comes in the name of the Lord! 10Blessed is the coming kingdom of our ancestor David! Hosanna in the highest heaven!"	1When they had come near Jerusalem and had reached Bethphage, at the Mount of Olives, Jesus sent two disciples, 2saying to them, "Go into the village ahead of you, and immediately you will find a donkey tied, and a colt with her; untie them and bring them to me. 3If anyone says anything to you, just say this, 'The Lord needs them.' And he will send them immediately." 4This took place to fulfill what had been spoken through the prophet, saying, 5"Tell the daughter of Zion, Look your king is coming to you, humble, and mounted on a donkey, and on a colt, the foal of a donkey." 6The disciples went and did as Jesus had directed them; 7they brought the donkey and the colt, and put their cloaks on them, and he sat on them. 8A very large crowd spread their cloaks on the road, and others cut branches from the trees and spread them on the road. 9The crowds that went ahead of him and that followed were shouting, "Hosanna, to the Son of David: Blessed is the one who comes in the name of the Lord! Hosanna in the highest heaven!"	29When he had come near Bethphage and Bethany, at the place called the Mount of Olives, he sent two of the disciples, 30saying, "Go into the village ahead of you, and as you enter it you will find tied there a colt that has never been ridden. Untie it and bring it here. 31If anyone asks you, 'Why are you untying it?' just say this, 'The Lord needs it'." Those who were sent departed and found it as he had told them. 33As they were untying the colt, its owners asked them, "Why are you untying the colt?" 34They said, "The Lord needs it." 35Then they brought it to Jesus; and after throwing their cloaks on the colt, they set Jesus on it. 36 As he rode along, people kept spreading their cloaks on the road. 37As he was now approaching the path down from the Mount of Olives, the whole multitude of the disciples began to praise God joyfully with a loud voice for all the deeds of power that they had seen, 38saying, "Blessed is the king who comes in the name of the Lord! Peace in heaven, and glory in the highest heaven!"

ing of his person and life as this was perceived by some of his contemporaries and early Christian believers.

IMPORTANCE OF THE JESUS OF HISTORY

The "Jesus of history" has been one of the major subjects of contemporary Christological investigation and New Testament studies. Almost every current work in Christology attempts to uncover the historical facts about Jesus, to extract what he actually said and did from the gospel presentations of the Christ of faith and the meaning of Jesus' life they put forward.

Why is this important? Of what significance is the Jesus of history? There are some who maintain that the historical Jesus is *not* important. What is important, they say, is the faith in Jesus found in the early church's understanding of what he meant. We can base our own faith reflections on that. Yet, although the early church's understanding of Jesus is indeed important, knowledge of the Jesus of history is likewise and in a crucial way important. It is important for a number of reasons. First, the search for the Jesus of history is a necessary search because of our present-day understanding of the gospels and how they developed. We simply cannot hold to the former understanding of the gospels, ignorant of the problem of the historical Jesus. The question of the historical Jesus is there; it must be addressed.

Second, the Jesus of history can serve as a "measuring stick," for developing Christian tradition. The Jesus of history can help keep ever before us the attitudes and ideals of Jesus that so influenced the early Christian tradition and its gospel presentation of Jesus. Christianity is based not on some timeless ideal, but on a concrete, historical person who spoke, taught, and did wondrous deeds. What he said and did are thus very relevant. The church, made up of human beings who are limited and historically conditioned, "infected" in various ways with Original Sin and thus subject to conscious and unconscious biases, will always have the need of making sure that what it says and does is consistent with or in the spirit of Jesus of Nazareth whom it proclaims as "God-with-us."

But the search for the Jesus of history is a difficult one. Was he really born in Bethlehem of the lineage of David or is this a construct of the early church, part of its conviction that Jesus was the Messiah who was supposed to be of David's lineage? Did he really perform miraculous cures? Did he really walk on water? Did he really say that he was "the way, the truth, and the life"? Did he really prohibit divorce (as in

Mark's gospel) or did he provide an exception (as in Matthew's gospel)? What did he *really* say and do? This is what the quest for the historical Jesus is concerned with.

CRITERIA OF AUTHENTICITY

In order to extract the Jesus of history from the Christ of faith presented in the gospels, a number of criteria are used that are part of the "modern historical methods" referred to earlier. There are four important and useful criteria.[2]

The first major criterion of authenticity is that of *embarrassment or contradiction*. This criterion takes seriously the sayings or actions of Jesus in the gospels that would have embarrassed or created some difficulty for the early church. The logic of this criterion is that the early church would not likely have created material that would embarrass the church or weaken its position with respect to opponents, or that would hinder the spreading of its message. It would be more likely for the early church to suppress or soften such material. Thus, material that tends to embarrass or weaken the church's position probably had its basis in actual, historical occurrences, things that happened in the life of Jesus, and is not constructed by the early church or the gospel writers.

The baptism of Jesus by John the Baptist is an example of this. It shows Jesus submitting to John while the early church was proclaiming Jesus' superiority over all the previous prophets, including John. Indeed, when we read the gospels, we see what appears to be a progressive attempt to weaken this rather embarrassing event. The first gospel, Mark's, simply recounts the event, giving no reason for it (see Mark 1:4–11). The second gospel written, Matthew's, presents John the Baptist admitting his unworthiness to baptize Jesus and relents only when Jesus commands him to do so, in that God's plans must thereby be fulfilled (see Matthew 3:13–17). Luke's gospel, the third, has the Baptist also admitting his unworthiness and talking about one who is greater than he is (see Luke 3:1–22). John's gospel has the Baptist admit his inferiority, but has no story of Jesus' being baptized (see John 1:29–34). It is quite unlikely that the early church created the story of the baptism of Jesus by John, and it seems that there was an attempt to explain it in a way favorable to Christianity (as in the case of Matthew and Luke) or to omit it altogether from the record (as in the case of John's gospel) in order to lessen the embarrassment.

This principle gives rise to the significant realization that there were indeed checks on the inventiveness of the early church and the gospel writers. The presence of embarrassing material like the baptism of Jesus by John, Peter's denial of Jesus, Jesus' crucifixion in the manner of a criminal execution, indicates a certain "conservative" check on the construction of Jesus' life. Historical fact, even embarrassing fact, was not always denied or suppressed.

A second criterion of authenticity is the criterion of *discontinuity*. This criterion centers on words or actions of Jesus that cannot be derived either from the Judaism of Jesus' time or from the early church. The logic of this focuses on the origin of such material. Two examples of discontinuity between Jesus and the Judaism of his day are the absolute prohibition of divorce in Mark 10:2–12, and Jesus' use of the word "abba" as a referent for God. These were both highly unusual, if not unique in Jesus' Jewish tradition. And neither serves to advance the interests of the early church. It seems most likely that they came from Jesus himself rather than from the faith-inspired inventiveness of the early church.

Of course, Jesus must have acted and spoken in a way quite continuous, or in line, with what others of his time were saying and doing, too. This principle by no means enables us to construct a complete picture of the historical Jesus; it simply notes what was unusual about him. Yet, along with the preceding criterion and the one that follows, it allows us to say a few things with some measure of certainty.

A third criterion of authenticity is that of *multiple attestation*. According to this criterion, sayings, actions, or themes that are found in more than one independent source (Mark, "Q," Paul, or John, for example) or more than one literary type (parable, miracle story, or dispute story) are likely to have a basis in the actual sayings and deeds of Jesus of Nazareth. If such sayings, actions, or themes crop up in unrelated sources or a number of literary types, it is unlikely that they were made up by the constructive tendencies of the early church. Examples of this are the marvelous deeds of healing and exorcism performed by Jesus, and the centrality of the approaching kingdom of God in his preaching and parables.

A final criterion is worth noting: *coherence*. This criterion says that sayings and deeds of Jesus that "fit in well" with sayings and deeds established as authentic by the other criteria have a good chance of having a basis in the actual sayings and deeds of Jesus, even though one cannot establish this by the other criteria. Thus, the parable of the Good Samaritan, found only in Luke's gospel, may indeed be a parable very close to what Jesus actually said since in its theme and in its style it is consistent with what one can determine about the Jesus of history by applying the other criteria.

A note of caution is in order at this point, relative to the use of these criteria. Those who use them do not claim that we can definitively say "Jesus said exactly *this*" or "Jesus did *this* in this place at this time." The claims made are much more modest. What we come up with is more the *typical sorts of things* Jesus said (the "voice" of Jesus rather than his very words), the *typical sorts of things he did*, and his *typical attitudes*. We can also come up with the general contours of his life and fate. Not everything about him can be known. Nonetheless, there *is* quite a substantial, if incomplete, portrait of him that *can* be drawn. The main features of this portrait will be drawn in the two chapters that follow.

NOTES
1. Quoted from John P. Meier, *A Marginal Jew: Rethinking the Historical Jesus,* Volume 1: *The Roots of the Problem and the Person* (New York: Doubleday, 1991), pp. 89-90.
    2. The following discussion relies heavily on Meier, *A Marginal Jew*, ch. 6.

QUESTIONS FOR REFLECTION AND DISCUSSION
1. What comes to mind when you think of Jesus? Make a list of your thoughts. Where have your ideas come from?
    2. Concerning the parallel gospel columns on page 95, make a list of the differences you notice among the three versions of the one event. Read the gospel of John and the gospel of Mark. Make a list of the more prominent similarities and differences that you notice.
    3. Explain the difference between the Christ of faith and the Jesus of history. What is your reaction to the distinction?
    4. "Jesus was a real human being, subject to the limits and historical conditioning that are part of all human existence." What is your reaction to this? Are you offended? Attracted? Explain.

SUGGESTED READING
Meier, John P. *A Marginal Jew: Rethinking the Historical Jesus.* Volume 1: *The Roots of the Problem and the Person.* Garden City, N.Y.: Doubleday, 1991. [Note: There is much written on the topic of the historical Jesus. This book by Meier is, by far, the best.]

McAteer, Michael R. and Michael S. Steinhauser. *The Man in the Scarlet Robe: Two Thousand Years of Searching for Jesus.* Toronto: United Church Publishing House, 1996.

CHAPTER ELEVEN

JESUS OF NAZARETH: MINISTRY AND TEACHING

W hat was Jesus like? What did he say and do? What were his attitudes? These are the sorts of questions contemporary theologians have been asking about Jesus as they pursue a Christology "from below." Have you ever thought about questions such as these? Many students are puzzled at these questions because they have presumed that we simply open up our gospels and there is Jesus. As explained in the previous chapter, we must answer these questions with the realization that the gospels are not exact historical records of Jesus' life. To come up with a portrait of the historical Jesus, we have to dig beneath the gospel text for answers to these questions by using the criteria of authenticity outlined in the previous chapter.

We must be cautious, however. When searching for the "Jesus of history," the subjective interest of the searcher always plays a role. There is no absolutely disinterested and neutral perspective because what the searcher discerns from among all the bits of factual data is a function in some way of his or her interests, concerns, or training. What the searcher sees as important, and especially the way he or she organizes the data, are dependent on conscious and unconscious "filters."

We can understand this by imagining we are taking a pet cat to see the veterinarian. When the cat is on the examination table, we see a poor, shaking creature that we must comfort. Because getting a needle or having its temperature taken is painful and distressing, our task is to console the animal; what we notice is its distress. The vet, for her part, sees a patient. She listens to the cat's heartbeat, reads its temperature, and feels for unusual growths on its body. She is looking for signs of pathology and will notice things that we cannot because she is trained to do so. What we see and the context from which we see depends on our particular perspective, a function of many things, such as our training and previous experience. It's the same cat, but viewed differently. The same is true of the data of Jesus' life. The portrait we paint will always reflect who we are and our particular concerns and background.

CENTRAL THEME OF JESUS' PREACHING

Jesus of Nazareth was a wandering preacher, a man who some time in his thirties started to preach and to teach, most likely in Galilee, the northern province of Israel, and also in Judea, the southern province in which the capital, Jerusalem, was located. He moved from town to town with a message that had a definite focus: the coming kingdom, or reign, of God. The next time you read the gospels, note how often "the kingdom of God" (or "the kingdom of heaven") appears. You will see that it occurs frequently in Jesus' teaching; it is a constant theme in his parables, and, as we shall soon see, it is key to understanding his marvelous deeds of healing and exorcising. The gospel of Mark (1:14–15) has a summary of Jesus' message, a summary that captures Jesus' very "voice":

> Now after John was arrested, Jesus came to Galilee, proclaiming the good news of God, and saying, "The time is fulfilled, and the kingdom of God has come near; repent, and believe in the good news."

What was this "kingdom of God" (or "kingdom of heaven" in Matthew's gospel) that Jesus talked about? Why was this "good news"? And, very important, how was Jesus connected with its coming? These are all important questions that arise as we put together our portrait of this man Jesus.

The phrase "kingdom of God," although not common in Jesus' day, was certainly not an incomprehensible phrase for Jesus' audience.[1] Its roots lay in the history of Israel when Israel began to define itself as a nation with a king, like other nations.[2] The real king was Yahweh, their

God; the earthly king was a kind of earthly proxy for God, ruling in God's place and in God's name.

Key to understanding Jesus' expression "the kingdom of God" is the Jewish expectation of God's coming to set things right once again. This expectation grew out of the failure of the kings of Israel to act like God's representatives and the experience of oppression that the Jewish people suffered from the hands of various occupying forces. In the fifth century B.C.E., the dynasty of David came to an end and with it Israel's monarchy and independence (except for a period of approximately 166–63 B.C.E.). In Jesus' day, the Romans were the occupying force. And so there was a longing for freedom—for salvation really— that in Jesus' time meant freedom from Roman rule. God would come, and Israel would be free.

Many Jews associated the coming of God to save Israel with the idea of a "Messiah." The term "messiah" comes from a Hebrew word meaning "the anointed one"; originally it referred simply to the king of Israel who was anointed as ruler over the people. The word *christos*, from which we derive our word "Christ," is the Greek equivalent. Over the course of time, the term had come to signify a future great king who would free Israel from its persecutors and establish a reign of justice and peace. This great king would be acting in God's name and with God's power. For most Jews, this Messiah would be of David's lineage, David being the greatest king in Jewish consciousness. For some Jews, however, the Messiah would not be a king but rather a great priest who would establish and preside over a cultic people, worshiping God in purity and in holiness.

In some Jewish circles, as part of all of the speculation about a Messiah and hopes for God's setting things aright, there was a lively apocalyptic mentality. This mentality involves a particular way of looking at world history and God's eventual saving action on behalf of the chosen people, Israel. It is characterized, first, by the abandonment of hope in the present situation. This world, as we now know it, is so much under the control of evil powers that it cannot be redeemed and made better. Salvation is possible only if God steps in, does away with the present world, and sets up an entirely new world. The apocalyptic mind, then, looked forward to a "new heaven and a new earth." The phrase "kingdom of God" was not normally an apocalyptic one, but could easily be a way of talking about this new situation. It is difficult to say how present this view of reality was during Jesus' time, but it was certainly there.

The destruction of the old world and the evil powers that control it would be accompanied by catastrophic events, in the apocalyptic mind. Descriptions of the end times abounded. The gospels themselves present us with rather typical descriptions of the end of the world that characterized apocalyptic writing. Mark's gospel (13:24–28), for example, has Jesus say about the end times:

> But in those days, after that suffering,
> the sun will be darkened,
> and the moon will not give its light,
> and the stars will be falling from heaven
> and the powers in the heavens will be shaken.
> Then they will see "the Son of Man coming in clouds" with great power and glory. Then he will send out the angels, and gather his elect from the four winds, from the ends of the earth to the ends of heaven.

This passage also indicates a number of other features of the apocalyptic view of things. The end of the world would be preceded by a heightening of suffering for the elect, the just ones. These sufferings were called the "eschatological woes" ("eschatological" means pertaining to the final things, the end time). The notion of the resurrection of the dead and a final judgment was part of apocalypticism, too. For some, all the dead would be raised and there would be a judgment, with the evildoers going to everlasting punishment and the just receiving an eternal reward. For others, only the just would be raised, to a glorious state.

In some of the apocalyptic speculation there was talk of an agent of God, a semi-divine figure, who would act in God's name in doing away with the present order and be the judge of the just and the unjust. This apocalyptic figure was named, by some, the "Son of Man."

There were other expectations connected to the end times and the coming of God that are worth noting. Some Jews expected God to send a kingly Messiah to turn out Israel's enemies and set up a peaceful order that would last for a period of time (how long was debated) before the end of this world as we know it. Others expected an "eschatological prophet," this is, a prophet of the end times who would announce the coming of the end to prepare the people for it. Still others thought that this prophet would be Elijah, returned from where God had "hidden" him. Elijah had not died, many thought, but had been swept away in a fiery chariot and would return to announce the end.[3]

In the midst of all of this expectation about the coming of God and perhaps the end of the world, Jesus began to preach that God was on the way, using the image of the kingdom of God. The time of salvation was "at hand"! This is important to keep in mind when it comes to understanding Jesus and his message. Statements such as the one from Mark's gospel, quoted just above, indicating the imminence of God's approach, most likely capture the belief of Jesus that the end was indeed near. It was not something in the far-off future. It would be highly unusual for the tradition of the early church to invent such an idea, especially because when the gospels were written the expectation of the imminent end of the world was waning. And such an expectation was indeed held by the early Christians, as the letters of Paul in the New Testament show.[4] It was, in fact, the delay of this end and the lessening of the tension created by its expectation that led to the writing of the gospels. Since the end had not come, and the original witnesses to Jesus' message were dying off, it became necessary to preserve his memory for the present and future generations of believers.

The kingdom was on its way, and in light of this Jesus urged his listeners to repent, to change their ways. There is a real urgency in his preaching. But what does this mean? How did one repent to prepare for the coming of God's kingdom, that situation of salvation and well-being?

THE COMMAND TO LOVE: JESUS' PREACHING

If anything can be gleaned from the gospels about the attitude that Jesus expected of those who listened to him, it is the primacy he placed on love. Jesus called on his Jewish audience to remember their own tradition: they were to love God with their whole heart and minds and souls, and their neighbors as themselves. Luke's gospel provides a scene that captures this:

> Just then a lawyer stood up to test Jesus. "Teacher," he said, "what must I do to inherit eternal life?" He said to him, "What is written in the law? What do you read there?" He answered, "You shall love the Lord your God with all your heart, and with all your soul, and with all your strength, and with all your mind; and your neighbor as yourself." And he said to him, "You have given the right answer; do this, and you will live."[5]

But what does it mean to love? For many, this word conjures up the idea of romantic affection. For others, it means sexual interaction. But for Jesus, it meant something different from these. Although he never really formally defined what he meant, his words, actions, and attitudes imaged what love involved. It is not too much to say that the love Jesus called for involved centering one's life trustingly on God and having concern for the well-being of others. But we can say more.

First of all, Jesus made the connection between love of God and love of neighbor. One cannot exist without the other. Therefore, acts of love are possible and necessary even on the sabbath, that holy day set aside in Jewish piety for rest and worship. Jesus thus cured people on the sabbath day, an action that many regarded as breaking the law of sabbath rest. People remembered that he even said that being at peace with our brother or sister was just as important as worship of God! In fact, we ought to delay such worship until reconciliation has taken place (see Matthew 5:23–24).

Second, there is a real radicalness to the sort of love that Jesus preached, a radicalness that expanded the boundaries of love in such a way as to make love unbounded, in effect. Read the parable of the "Good Samaritan" (Luke 10:29–37). This is a parable that deals with the question "Who is my neighbor?" the neighbor I must love. The neighbor to be loved, in this parable, is the Samaritan, a shocking element in the story to most of Jesus' audience since Samaritans and Jews were enemies and had been engaged for centuries in a bitter religious and social rivalry. Jesus is telling his listeners that even the hated one, the enemy, is to be loved!

This unbounded love is also captured in Matthew's remembrances of Jesus' preaching. Matthew gathers a number of Jesus' sayings and places them together in the so-called Sermon on the Mount (5:43–47):

"You have heard that it was said, 'You shall love your neighbor and hate your enemy.' But I say to you, love your enemies and pray for those who persecute you, so that you may be children of your Father in heaven; for he makes his sun rise on the evil and on the good, and sends rain on the righteous and on the unrighteous. For if you love those who love you, what reward do you have? Do not even the tax collectors do the same? And if you greet only your brothers and sisters, what more are you doing than others? Do not even the Gentiles do the same?"

THE COMMAND TO LOVE: JESUS' ACTIONS

Jesus' actions indicate, as well, dimensions of the radical understanding he had of loving others. His understanding of what love meant involved a radical inclusiveness. Thus, Jesus reached out especially to the outcasts of society, persons who, because of their moral laxity or sinfulness or because of physical ailments, were alienated from "acceptable" society. One of the most frequent groups of "sinners" with whom Jesus had dealings were the tax collectors. These men had two strikes against them. They were considered as thieves because they often extorted from their compatriot Jews far more than the Romans demanded they gather in taxes. They were also seen as traitors because they were working for the Roman oppressors and hence against God's chosen people. On both accounts, they were sinners and outcasts. But Jesus ate with them, an action that was, and still is, symbolic of a kind of reconciliation and companionship. Indeed, these meals symbolized for Jesus the messianic banquet of God's rule, the good times that were coming. Jesus was announcing that God's kingdom was available to them, too, and he was symbolically acting this out since the image of a heavenly banquet was one of the images of the salvation to come. Sinners were not outcasts; God sought reconciliation with them.

Jesus associated with another group of outcasts, too: lepers. Leprosy in the Bible is a term used to include a great variety of skin diseases; it does not necessarily mean leprosy in the medical sense we use it today. The contracting of any of these diseases rendered a person "unclean" and resulted in being excluded from society. Persons with such diseases, moreover, were "religiously" unclean and so there was a double impurity that characterized their state and made them outcasts. Jesus, however, did not drive them away when they sought him. He did not denounce them as impure; he cured them. The well-being that was characteristic of God's rule and the inclusive nature of love encircled even these feared outcasts.

Jesus' association with women is yet another indication of the nature of love that Jesus preached and enacted. His attitude toward women was highly unusual for a man of his day. Women were among his followers, something that did not happen in rabbinical circles where the students were all male. In fact, women were not allowed to participate fully in the Jewish religious observances as men were, and certainly had no real say or presence in the Jewish religious leadership. In a very well-known story, Jesus commends Mary who is listening to him and learning from him—being a disciple, in other words—when Mary is criticized by her sister Martha for not doing the traditional womanly things around the house (Luke 10:38–42). In Jesus' understanding of love, what we today call the patriarchal power structures are not to be maintained, power structures that assigned particular roles for women and men and effectively subordinated women to men. This hierarchical order in which some dominate and control others is not part of the pattern of relationships that ought to characterize the reign of God. Truly loving relationships under God's rule involve very different patterns of social relationships and very different social structures.

God of the Kingdom

Jesus' understanding of love and the values and attitudes he made real in his own life were undoubtedly based upon his experience and understanding of the God whose reign was nearing. The gospels do not provide us with any details of the actual experience of God or the moment it occurred that led Jesus to begin his preaching and teaching ministry. They do, however, indicate what to Jesus were the essential characteristics of his God.

This God was the God, first of all, of Jesus' Jewish heritage, the God who, for Jews, had chosen them above all others to be a special people witnessing to this great and only God. This God had freed their ancestors from slavery in Egypt, had established a special covenant relationship with them, and had given them the Law (Torah) through Moses. This God had given them the Promised Land of Israel, but had punished them for their sinfulness. This was a God who cared for them and who loved them.

Jesus' understanding of God built upon this heritage and gave it special twists. In many ways, this God was, in Jesus' view, a rather strange God, at least when compared to people's expectations. This God was, for example, like a shepherd who goes out and seeks the lost sheep, leaving the other sheep alone in their pen. This God *cares for sinners* and *actively* goes out to seek them (Luke 15:3–7; Matthew 18:12–14). God was a God who unexpectedly and generously *forgives* and accepts sinners *without demanding justice* or recompense (Luke 15:11–32). This God was a God of unexpected, even "offensive" *generosity* (Matthew 20:1–16). A God of compassion, mercy, forgiveness, who desires the well-being of all and goes out to sinners and outcasts, a God who is not bound to the order of strict justice—*this* is the God

Jesus talked about. Indeed, so close and affectionate was this God that Jesus could call God "Abba" ("Daddy"), a Jewish term of endearment that evoked feelings of warmth and intimacy, a term not used by Jesus' contemporaries in their talk about God.

MIRACLES OF JESUS

The gospel tradition is full of stories about Jesus' amazing acts of healing and exorcisms, and even other acts, such as the feeding of the five thousand, walking on water, and causing a fig tree to wither. What is your attitude toward these? Do you think such events are possible? These "miraculous" events are the source of much skepticism today because our culture with its understanding of reality has little or no use for the miraculous, understood as the supernatural breaking of the laws of nature. Yet the miracle tradition is so embedded in the gospels that to remove it would seriously undermine their credibility and, indeed, take away significant portions of the Jesus story.

That Jesus performed marvelous, extraordinary feats of healing and that people saw him "casting out devils" cannot be denied. As well as being so integral to the gospel stories about Jesus, these feats are attested to in various independent sources (Mark, "Q," Matthew, Luke, John, and Paul all talk about these marvels) and so, they must have an historical basis to them. One must expect, however, that these stories have been embellished and their miraculous nature exaggerated at times. One must also expect purely legendary stories of miracles to have spread and become part of the gospel tradition.

HOW DOES GOD ACT IN THE WORLD?

The question of the miracles of Jesus touches upon the question of how God acts in the world. It is useful at this point to make a slight detour on this issue because of its importance. There are two positions on the extremes. The first is a supernaturalist position, which sees God breaking arbitrarily into nature and doing things that break the patterns of nature and are physically impossible. An airplane plummeting nose first and out of control toward the ground that simply stops just before hitting the ground and settles gently down, without the pilot or any other natural force doing anything, would be an example. The second extreme is a naturalist position, which denies that God acts at all in the world. In this view, God may have created the world, but, like a person who winds up a clock and lets it go, God has nothing more to do with the world. God starts the whole process and then retires, allow-ing it to go on its way unhindered. The first position is one that many would think a religious person ought to have. Many students are quite surprised, even shocked, when it is suggested that there may be another way of looking at things that denies the supernaturalist position.

Although there is debate about this, there are theologians who say that we are actually being true to our real experience to deny that supernatural miracles, understood as events that break the laws of nature, take place. There are amazing events that do happen. People are healed unexpectedly against all odds, for example. But divine intervention that breaks the patterns of nature is not the explanation that springs to mind as the only possible solution. We are, in our culture, used to looking for "natural" solutions, even to the most amazing occurrences. A marvelous cure may be the result of psychosomatic forces at work, or the result of some natural agent that we have overlooked or whose existence we are, at present, ignorant of. This does not, of course, mean that a supernatural event has not occurred. Yet, these theologians are satisfied with this approach, saying that recourse to the supernatural reflects a premodern time when people had no other explanations.

Does this not, then, deny God's presence and activity? Not necessarily. Rather than experiencing God as "outside" and stepping in, it might be better to see God as affecting us from within the events of our lives. We might think of God at work calling us in and through our experiences to act justly or to work for peace and love. Experiencing the life of a Mother Teresa, for example, may trigger an experience of a call to act like she does. Or, our experience of injustice might engender in us a sense of outrage and a desire to correct it. In all of this, we are experiencing the presence and activity of God, calling us to live our lives in a particular way, giving them a particular direction. Christians would experience God at work calling them to make real the values and attitudes of Jesus. He provides the focal point for understanding what God calls us to, from within our experience. The point is that God is at work not breaking in from the outside, but rather from within the experience we have as a "depth" dimension to it. God is not absent!

Meaning of Jesus' Miracles

If we return to the miracle stories in the gospels, the most common ones are healings and exorcisms. The other miracles, the so-called nature miracles (walking on water, cursing a fig tree), are more problematic and might more easily be thought of as legendary in their origins. But it is virtually certain that people saw Jesus perform amazing acts of healing, and saw Jesus cast out devils. Today, however, we may explain these events differently than Jesus' contemporaries did; we may have recourse to psychosomatic healing or attribute some psychological problem to those described as demon-possessed. Nonetheless, the meaning of these marvelous deeds of Jesus is a key question because they provide us with further insight into his mission and how he understood his role. Both Matthew and Luke include an episode from "Q" that points us in the right direction. Here is Luke's version (11:14–20):

> Now he was casting out a demon that was mute; when the demon had gone out, the one who had been mute spoke, and the crowds were amazed. But some of them said, "He casts out demons by Beelzebul, the ruler of the demons." Others, to test him, kept demanding from him a sign from heaven. But he knew what they were thinking and said to them, "Every kingdom divided against itself becomes a desert, and house falls on house. If Satan also is divided against himself, how will his kingdom stand?—for you say that I cast out the demons by Beelzebul. Now if I cast out the demons by Beelzebul, by whom do your exorcists cast them out? Therefore they will be your judges. But if it is by the finger of God that I cast out demons, then the kingdom of God has come to you."

It is the last sentence that provides the clue. The miracle tradition is tied to the central theme of Jesus' preaching: the coming rule of God. Indeed, as the story indicates, the marvelous wonders are signs that God's rule is being established, and it is being established in and through Jesus' actions. He is no mere prophet announcing that the reign of God is near; he is the agent of its being made real. The underlying logic of the connection of the miracles and the coming of the kingdom is quite simple: God's reign means human well-being. When God's reign approaches—indeed, when God's reign is established—all manner of human oppression, including sickness, is done away with. God's reign means salvation for human beings, salvation in all of its aspects.

The kingdom of God was nearing; repent and believe this good news! Such was the essential message of Jesus, a message he preached and the implications of which he lived out in his dealings with others.

Yet not everyone embraced this message with joy. It did not appear to be good news. We must now turn to Jesus' tragic fate.

NOTES

1. See the excellent discussion in John P. Meier, *A Marginal Jew: Rethinking the Historical Jesus*. Volume 2: *Mentor, Message, and Miracles* (New York: Doubleday, 1994), ch. 14.

2. See the story of this in 1 & 2 Samuel, and the history of Israel as a kingdom on the two parallel accounts, 1 & 2 Kings and 1 & 2 Chronicles.

3. See 2 Kings 2:1–12.

4. See, for example, 1 Corinthians 7:25–31.

5. Luke 10:25–28. See also Matthew 22:34–40, where Jesus, not the lawyer, enunciates these double "loves," and Mark 12:28–34. Both of these commandments can be found in the Jewish Torah and would have been known to Jesus' Jewish audience. The first one comes from Deuteronomy 6:4–5: "Hear, O Israel, the Lord is our God, the Lord alone. You shall love the Lord your God with all your heart, and with all your soul, and with all your might." The second one is found in Leviticus 19:18: "You shall not take vengeance or bear a grudge against any of your people, but you shall love your neighbor as yourself: I am the Lord."

QUESTIONS FOR REFLECTION AND DISCUSSION

1. Write out the understanding of Jesus' message you had before reading this chapter. Compare and/or contrast it with what this chapter says.

2. Do you believe in miracles? Explain your belief. What do you think of the ideas about miracles set forth in this chapter?

3. Read over the parable of the Prodigal Son in Luke 15:11–32. What does this parable tell us about how God acts toward us? Is it consistent with what you have been told about God or with your image of God? Elaborate.

4. "Jesus embodied the God of the kingdom in his actions and attitudes." What is there in Jesus' life that would support this?

SUGGESTED READINGS

Johnson, Elizabeth A. *Consider Jesus: Waves of Renewal in Christology*, chapters 2, 3, and 4. New York: Crossroad, 1990.

Küng, Hans. *On Being a Christian*, pp. 214–277. Translated by Edward Quinn. Garden City, N.Y.: Doubleday, 1976.

Meier, John P. *A Marginal Jew: Rethinking the Historical Jesus*. Volume 2: *Mentor, Message, and Miracles*. Garden City, N.Y.: Doubleday, 1994.

This book is quite detailed but not impossible to read. It is by far the best treatment of this topic I have encountered.

O'Collins, Gerald. *Interpreting Jesus*, chapters 1 and 2. Mahwah, N.J.: Paulist Press, 1983.

CHAPTER TWELVE

THE DEATH OF JESUS

I f you glance around a room in a Catholic hospital or school, or enter a church of almost any Christian denomination, chances are that you will see a crucifix or a cross hanging on a wall. The crucifix reminds us of the type of death that Jesus suffered: he was executed in the way the Romans of his day commonly executed non-Roman criminals and persons charged with sedition. Have you ever thought about this, that Jesus was executed as a criminal? Why did Jesus suffer this fate? What was there about him that caused such a lethal reaction? After all, he was preaching a message of love and inclusion. What was so offensive about that?

OPPOSITION TO JESUS

There certainly was offense at Jesus' ministry. Even a cursory reading of the gospels reveals an opposition to what he was doing. Most of it came from those whom the gospels refer to as scribes and Pharisees. And then there was the important group in Jerusalem, the Sanhedrin, the supreme Jewish legal and religious body, which was most immediately involved in the condemnation of Jesus to death.

The scribes were the professional theologians of Jesus' day, men trained in the written Law upon which Jewish religious thought and practice were based, and in the extensive oral commentary on this Law that had developed. This Law was coextensive with the Pentateuch, the first five books of the Jewish Scriptures (equivalent to the first five books of the Old Testament). It was deemed to have come from God through Moses. The Pharisees, for their part, formed a distinctive religious movement in Judaism and were men noted for their rigorous obedience to the Law. Many scribes belonged to this movement. This zealousness for the Law, characteristic of the scribes and the Pharisees, is an important factor in understanding the opposition to Jesus.

Another group deserves mention: the Sadducees. This was a group comprised mainly of the priestly families and lay aristocracy centered in Jerusalem. One of the ways in which they differed from the Pharisees was that they rejected the notion of the resurrection from the dead. In general, members of this religious group tended to want to make accommodations as much as possible with the Romans. In effect, they had made their peace with the Roman occupation of Palestine and directed their efforts to benefiting from it. Theirs was not a revolutionary spirit. This group held the balance of power in the Sanhedrin when Jesus was alive.

But why would these groups be offended by Jesus? Part of the answer lies in the criticism, both explicit and implicit, that he leveled by his words and actions at many of their social and religious views. Jesus was no innocuous and accommodating preacher. He upset many people because he was, in effect, challenging their worldview and the religious convictions that were so much a part of it. His radical, inclusive love, for example, was a real challenge and affront to the expectations of most of the people of his day (as it still is in our day). Love of enemies, unusual associations with women, the inclusion of sinners and outcasts—this pointed to a new world order.

This should not be minimized. Don't we humans have a propensity for order and the security that accompanies it, or seems to? Don't we resist any threat to this order, even when it may be an order that oppresses people? It is threatening to step into the unknown, even when the unknown offers possibilities for betterment. Even slaves can be afraid of freedom. Of course, those who benefit from the established order are most threatened. Whether it is the former apartheid government in South Africa putting down resistance to the established order, or English and American governments resisting granting the vote to women at the beginning of this century, the history of the human race is filled with examples of the reactions of those who strike out against change—almost *any* change—that threatens the way things are. You may be able to think of examples in your own life of times when you were upset because of someone else's "unorthodox" views. Or you may think of situations or events that made you question the world you know and want to remain. A homeless person on the street asking for money can upset our comfortable world.

Jesus' reaching out to those who were considered sinners and outcasts was something that threatened the established order and people's expectations. This resulted in a reaction of disapproval from the religious leaders, or some of them, at any rate. An incident from Luke's gospel (19:1–7) will illustrate this typical reaction.

> [Jesus] entered Jericho and was passing through it. A man was there named Zacchaeus; he was a chief tax collector and was rich. He was trying to see who Jesus was, but on account of the crowd he could not, because he was short in stature. So he ran ahead and climbed a sycamore tree to see him, because he was going to pass that way. When Jesus came to the place, he looked up and said to him, "Zacchaeus, hurry and come down; for I must stay at your house today." So he hurried down and was happy to welcome him. All who saw it began to grumble and said, "He has gone to be the guest of one who is a sinner."

The despised tax collector was welcomed by Jesus; the lost one was sought out, not excluded. God's love and mercy was being extended even to a sinner. The reaction of the onlookers is not unusual. Think about your own reaction to someone you regard as a sinner or socially unacceptable. Picture that person. Can you imagine sitting down at table with him or her?

Jesus' challenge to the established conventions, enough in itself to provoke an angry reaction, was accompanied by a great sense of authority, composure, and self-assurance; the gospels all show that Jesus struck people as being a man *with authority*. A rather typical description occurs in Mark 1:21–22: "They went to Capernaum; and when the sabbath came, he entered the synagogue and taught. They were astounded at his teaching, for he taught them as one having authority: and not as the scribes." When one reads the gospels, one is indeed struck by the fact that Jesus does not use previous, accepted authorities to back up his position. He speaks with a conviction of personal authority. "Amen, *I* say to you . . ." This conviction of his personal authority is especially evident in his attitude toward and treatment of the Jewish Law, the foundation of Jewish life and practice.

The Law, with all its moral and religious prescription, was not obeyed rigorously by all Jews. Those Jews living in Galilee, for example, far from Jerusalem, the religious center, were often regarded by the religious leaders with no small contempt because Galileans had a reputation for laxity. Jesus himself does not appear to have given the Law the absolute authority that many pious Pharisees and Sadducees did. In fact, one of the major complaints against him that surfaces in the gospels is precisely his lax attitude toward the Law. And the typical law that Jesus broke, according to the gospels, is the law of the sabbath rest. The following scene from Mark's gospel (3:1–6) is quite representative.

> Again he entered the synagogue, and a man was there who had a withered hand. They watched him to see whether he would cure him on the sabbath, so that they might accuse him. And he said to the man who had the withered hand, "Come forward." Then he said to them, "Is it lawful to do good or to do harm on the sabbath, to save life or to kill?" But they were silent. He looked around at them with anger; he was grieved at their hardness of heart and said to the man, "Stretch out your hand." He stretched it out, and his hand was restored. The Pharisees went out and immediately conspired with the Herodians against him, how to destroy him.

As many of the gospel stories of Jesus' healings show, healing on the sabbath was considered to be a breaking of the sabbath law of rest (which, to repeat, was considered to be God's law). Jesus knew what he was doing. He was indeed breaking this law. His motive, from all we can tell, was that of responding to a real human need that confronted him in the here and now. The well-being of humans took precedence over this law. What is crucial to realize is that Jesus felt that he had the *authority* to do this. He had authority even over a law that was deemed to have come from God! Here was a human being carrying out activity contrary to what was expected of Jews and placing himself above God's law. The charges that were laid against him later by those for whom the Law was so important, that he was a heretic and blasphemer, certainly have grounds.

Jesus' *teachings* and the authority with which he uttered them also served to elicit this negative reaction. Jesus dared to *correct* the Law and its customary interpretations in the Jewish tradition. The famous Sermon on the Mount shows this very well. Two examples (Matthew 5:21–22 and 5:38–42) will illustrate this.

"You have heard that it was said to those of ancient times, 'You shall not murder'; and 'whoever murders shall be liable to judgment.' But I say to you that if you are angry with a brother or sister, you will be liable to judgment; and if you insult a brother or sister, you will be liable to the council; and if you say, 'You fool,' you will be liable to the hell of fire."

"You have heard that it was said, 'An eye for an eye and a tooth for a tooth.' But I say to you, Do not resist an evildoer. But if anyone strikes you on the right cheek, turn the other also; and if anyone wants to sue you and take your coat, give your cloak as well; and if anyone forces you to go one mile, go also the second mile. Give to anyone who begs from you, and do not refuse anyone who wants to borrow from you."

Jesus' authority and its implications are also evident in a remembered incident concerning the forgiveness of sins. He tells a paralytic, in Luke's gospel, that his sins are forgiven, and the reaction is one of amazement and outrage, at least on the part of the religious leaders. Thus, in response to the assurance that the man's sins are forgiven, the lawyers and the Pharisees say: "Who is this who is speaking blasphemies? Who can forgive sins but God alone?" (Luke 5:21)

In trying to understand the hostility that Jesus provoked, a hostility that led some of the Jewish religious leaders to want to do away with him, we must take seriously the offense to the very basis of the Jewish religious tradition that was inherent in Jesus' message and activity, which the statements above capture. He was not only an "odd" person, associating with unusual people and outcasts. He was, in fact, offering a profound challenge to the acceptable ways of understanding God and responding religiously to God. He was a true heretic, leading people away from "true religion"; he was also a blasphemer in the sense that he was taking on for himself what belonged to God. Such persons are not well received. The Middle Ages had the Inquisition to persecute those judged to be heretics by orthodox Christianity. Think of the author Salman Rushdie. So-called fundamentalist Muslims have put a price on his life because they consider his book, *The Satanic Verses*, to have blasphemed. The reaction to Jesus is quite understandable and believable. What he was saying and doing was so offensive that it led to his death.

And then there were the Sadducees in Jerusalem, who held the balance of power in the Sanhedrin. This group seems to have most immediately brought about Jesus' death. As well as the reasons for opposing Jesus given above, they would have had another reason for wanting to do away with him: Jesus was causing unrest and was perceived as a threat to the good order under Roman rule to which they had accommodated themselves. This reconstruction is highly plausible given the disturbance Jesus caused when he drove out the money changers from the Temple in Jerusalem, an incident all four gospels recount. Mark's version describes the reaction of the Jerusalem leaders as follows (Mark 11:18): "And when the chief priests and the scribes heard it, they kept looking for a way to kill him; for they were afraid of him, because the whole crowd was spellbound by his teaching."

If the angry response to Jesus on the part of some, if not many, of the Jewish religious leaders is understandable, is the reaction of Pilate to Jesus understandable? Jesus was executed by the Romans after the manner of a Roman execution of subversives and criminals: crucifixion. All the gospels agree that there was some sort of trial or hearing before the Roman procurator in charge of Palestine at that time, Pontius Pilate, and that he either passed judgment on Jesus or allowed Jesus to be executed. Why?

The gospels provide a clue in the charge, hung on his cross, for which Jesus was executed: "Jesus of Nazareth, King of the Jews." The expression "King of the Jews" was one of those code words for "Messiah," which for the Romans would only mean a political agitator who would lead an uprising against the Roman rule of the land. There were grounds in Jesus' ministry for this charge, at least for someone who only heard about it from a distance. Jesus was talking about the coming reign of God. There were rumors, apparently, that he was the Messiah. The story of his triumphant entry into Jerusalem, and the gathering of a large crowd that accompanied it, would certainly make Pilate uneasy, especially in the midst of Jewish resentment of the Romans and the political murders that were carried out against the Romans and their collaborators by people known as Zealots. What is more, Jesus was in Jerusalem during the time of Passover when there were more Jews than normal in the city to celebrate this feast, and when religious fervor could easily boil over into social unrest. Pilate, it seems, had Jesus put to death, or at least agreed to go along with it, because he feared him as a messianic pretender and because he did not want to allow any trouble to occur during this sensitive time.

Jesus' Understanding of His Fate

It is most difficult to know what was going on in Jesus' mind as the hostility to his mission became more and more apparent and intense. Jesus must have recognized what was going on and he must have had some thoughts as to his fate. The gospels provide a number of interpretations. These may reflect views that Jesus held at times during his ministry, although they may also be simply interpretations of Jesus' fate that the later Christian communities superimposed on his life.

One such understanding is that of a rejected and persecuted prophet. In a "Q" saying (Matthew 23:37), Jesus is presented as referring to this. He cries: "Jerusalem, Jerusalem, the city that kills the prophets and stones those who are sent to it!" Could this be capturing Jesus referring to himself here, and not simply commenting on a tradition of rejected prophets? It is possible that Jesus understood his rejection in these terms.

The stories of the death of Jesus on the cross point to another understanding: that of the persecuted righteous person. There had emerged in the Jewish tradition the figure of a just person who is persecuted by sinners because his upright way of life is an affront to their evil ways (a perfectly understandable reaction with a lot of historical examples!). Psalm 22 is a classic example of this, one that is worth quoting from because it parallels so closely the depiction of Jesus' crucifixion in the gospels.

> My God, my God, why have you forsaken me?
>   Why are you so far from helping me,
>   from the words of my groaning?
> O my God, I cry by day, but you do not answer;
>   and by night, but find no rest.
>
> But I am a worm, and not human;
>   scorned by others, and despised by the people.
> All who see me mock at me;
>   they make mouths at me, they shake their heads;
> "Commit your cause to the Lord; let him deliver —
>   let him rescue the one in whom he delights!"
>
> For dogs are all around me;
>   a company of evildoers encircles me.
> My hands and feet have shriveled;

I can count all my bones.
They stare and gloat over me;
they divide my clothes among themselves,
    and for my clothing they cast lots.

It is hard to resist the temptation to think that the details of the story of Jesus' crucifixion depend on this psalm and that there has been an intent to portray Jesus as the suffering righteous one, but ultimately vindicated by God. It is conceivable that Jesus thought of his fate in this way, too, since it was a model he would have known. But it is very difficult to tell historically whether the gospels are constructing this interpretation of Jesus or whether it has roots in the attitudes of Jesus himself.

By far the best known interpretation of Jesus' death, however, is that Jesus' death is an atoning death, one that makes up for the sins of others. Jesus is quoted in a number of places as giving this interpretation of his fate. Thus, Matthew, in his description of the final meal Jesus had with his close disciples, describes Jesus as anticipating his fate and giving it this atoning significance. Matthew (26:27–28) has Jesus say, as he gives the cup of wine to his disciples: "Drink from it all of you; for this is the blood of the covenant, which is poured out for many for the forgiveness of sins."

This idea of righteous persons suffering death to bring about forgiveness of sins and healing for others had precedents in Jesus' heritage. One of these is the fourth song of the servant of Yahweh, found in Isaiah, chapters 52–53. This song celebrates the sufferings of a just servant of God, the servant probably representing an ideal people of Israel. His sufferings result in forgiveness and health—salvation, in other words. The death of Jewish martyrs, too, during the Jewish uprising against the Seleucid king, Antiochus IV, in the second century B.C.E., was considered to be a healing death for the nation. Thus, 2 Maccabees 7:37–38 quotes a person soon to be martyred:

"I, like my brothers, give up body and life for the laws of our ancestors, appealing to God to show mercy soon to our nation and by trials and plagues to make you confess that God alone is God, and through me and my brothers to bring to an end the wrath of the Almighty that has justly fallen on our whole nation."

There is yet another possible way of approaching this idea. It connects with the apocalyptic notion of the eschatological woes, mentioned in Chapter 11. In this scenario, before the end, there would be terrible suffering for the just. It is possible that Jesus connected his death with these woes. Indeed, it is possible that his suffering, the fate he could envision, became for him the eschatological woes that would then be followed by the end of the world and the coming of salvation. In this apocalyptic framework, Jesus' sufferings coincide with the establishment of the new covenant, that new situation of salvation.

Whatever the case may be, the gospel tradition picks up this idea of the sufferings of the just leading to salvation and applies it to Jesus. And indeed, Jesus himself may have interpreted his fate in this way because that would explain why it became so dominant in the later Christian Tradition. In his book *Interpreting Jesus*, Gerald O'Collins puts the matter this way:

> How can we account for this understanding of Jesus' crucifixion as "the universal vicarious atoning death of the Messiah" (Hengel, *The Atonement*, p. 71)? Would the disciples' encounters with the risen Jesus *alone* have been sufficient to trigger off this interpretation? It would have been enough to have taken the resurrection simply to mean that Jesus had been vindicated by God as a prophetic martyr or an innocent sufferer (Wisdom 2–5; Revelation 1:11f.). But the early Christians went much further than that in recognizing Jesus' crucifixion to be the representative death of the Messiah which atoned for human sin. They could hardly have done so, *unless the earthly Jesus had already in some way claimed to be Messiah and indicated that his coming death would have such an atoning value.*[1]

In any event, Jesus was put to death as an archheretic, a blasphemer, and a perceived threat to the established order. And that seemed to be the end of him. His followers, even, seem to have left and given up their hope in him and his cause. The gospels all indicate fear, disappointment, and disillusionment, not persistent and strong faith in him when he was crucified. But then something happened. This something was the resurrection. It is to this event and the historical discussions surrounding it that we must now turn.

NOTE

1. Gerald O'Collins, *Interpreting Jesus* (Mahwah, N.J.: Paulist, 1983), p. 92.

QUESTIONS FOR REFLECTION AND DISCUSSION

1. The death of Jesus was an intrinsic consequence of his life and preaching. Explain.

2. Reflect upon the world today. Can you identify any current examples of a person or group being persecuted because they offer a critique of the "way things are"? Who are they?

3. Think of your understanding of why Jesus was put to death. Does it differ from the reasons given in this chapter? How?

4. Jesus may have thought of his death as one that atoned for the sins of others. Discuss this idea of an atoning death. Does it make sense to you? Explain.

SUGGESTED READINGS

Hellwig, Monika K. *Jesus, the Compassion of God*, chapter 6. Wilmington, Delaware: Michael Glazier, 1983.

Hill, Brennan. *Jesus, the Christ: Contemporary Perspectives*, chapter 8. Mystic, Conn: Twenty-Third Publications, 1991.

Küng, Hans. *On Being A Christian*, pp. 278-342. Translated by Edward Quinn. Garden City, N.Y.: Doubleday, 1976.

O'Collins, Gerald. *Interpreting Jesus*, chapter 3. Mahwah, N.J.: Paulist, 1983.

CHAPTER THIRTEEN

THE RESURRECTION
OF JESUS

S ome time after the crucifixion of Jesus, a number of his followers began to claim that God had raised him from the dead and that he would soon return as judge of the living and the dead. The final day was near. Filled with the conviction that this was so, preachers traveled throughout much of the Roman Empire, preaching the resurrection as part of their message. A new religious movement, Christianity, had begun.

What about this claim that Jesus was raised from the dead? What does it mean? For many in our culture today, it is a fabrication, pure and simple. Rising from the dead? Impossible! It flies in the face of all we know about human life. It defies our understanding of biological processes. What about you? Do you think that the claim of Jesus' resurrection is a believable one? What comes to your mind when you think of it? Do you think of a corpse resuscitated? Or do you not think about it much because it is such an odd claim?

JEWISH UNDERSTANDING OF RESURRECTION
The idea that there will be a resurrection of the dead followed by a judgment has its roots in the apocalyptic understanding of reality and in the Jewish understanding of what was necessary if there is to be a real human life. In Jewish thinking, the idea that the dead would be raised to life surfaced some two hundred years before the birth of

Jesus. It was still a debatable belief in Jesus' day. That group of Jews called the Sadducees did not believe in a resurrection at all. This world and this life were all there was for them. Many Jews, however, including the Pharisees, did believe in a resurrection, a resurrection of the body to eternal life (or to punishment). The Jewish understanding of reality, unlike the Hellenistic one (a word referring to the predominant Greek tradition and culture of the time), did not conceive of an existence without some sort of "body." Greeks could think of a disembodied "soul" existing without a body forever, but Jewish ways of thinking required some form of body if there were to be an ongoing existence of an individual. At the end of this world, then, there would be a general resurrection followed by a judgment.

There was speculation as to what sort of "body" people would have in this new life. For some, it would be like the present body humans had in this world, but most believed that the resurrected body would be a *transformed* type of body, even a kind of "spiritual" body. The important New Testament writer Paul addresses this question in his first letter to the church at Corinth. He writes (15:42–44), concerning the resurrected body Christians will have:

> What is sown is perishable, what is raised is imperishable. It is sown in dishonor, it is raised in glory. It is sown in weakness, it is raised in power. It is sown a physical body, it is raised a spiritual body. If there is a physical body, there is also a spiritual body.

THE NEW TESTAMENT WITNESS

In the books of the New Testament, there is no description of the resurrection of Jesus itself. What we find are claims that Jesus has been raised, lists of persons to whom Jesus appeared, stories of Jesus' appearances, and stories of finding the tomb of Jesus empty.

The earliest surviving written testimony to the resurrection appears in Paul's first letter to the Corinthians (15:3–8), written in the early 50s C.E. Paul records a tradition he received about the resurrection.

> For I handed on to you as of first importance what I in turn had received: that Christ died for our sins in accordance with the scriptures, and that he was buried, and that he was raised on the third day in accordance with the scriptures, and that he appeared to Cephas, then to the twelve. Then he appeared to more than five hundred brothers and sisters at one time, most of whom are

still alive, though some have died. Then he appeared to James, then to all the apostles. Last of all, as to one untimely born, he appeared also to me.

You will note that this is simply a list of people Christ appeared to. There is no elaborate story of any of the appearances, and no mention of the finding of an empty tomb.

The gospels, written after Paul's letter and after some further circulation of stories about Jesus' resurrection and appearances, do provide details about the appearances. But biblical scholars by and large do not think that these appearance stories are factual descriptions of what took place. They are the result of the constructive storytelling of the early Christian Tradition and of the gospel writers.

Is this surprising? Many college students hear this for the first time in class; nothing in their religious education prepares them for it. It is impossible to review here all the sophisticated biblical work that lies behind this understanding, but as an example of the kind of clues that are in the gospel appearance stories that lead scholars to say this, consider the following. If you look at the ending of Matthew's gospel (28:16–20), you will see the story of Jesus appearing to the Eleven who had been his closest associates (without Judas, who had betrayed him). He tells them to go to all nations and baptize the people everywhere, making them disciples. Yet when you read the Acts of the Apostles, and indeed the various early Christian letters of the New Testament, there is no mention of missionary work being carried on by this group. Only Peter leaves Palestine (see Galatians 2:11, for example, where he goes to Antioch). It seems, in fact, that the Eleven did not engage in missionary work to all nations. Why not, if the disciples had, indeed, received the clear mandate that Matthew's gospel indicates?

Look at another clue, dealing with where the appearances took place. Luke's gospel has Jesus appear to the disciples only in and around Jerusalem. Indeed, Luke 24:50–51 shows Jesus ascending into heaven from Bethany, near Jerusalem, *on the same night* he rose from the dead. There are no Galilean appearances at all. Yet in Mark 16:7 and Matthew 28:7, an angel directs the disciples to go to Galilee where they will see Jesus. And it is there that they see him *for the first time*. Inconsistencies like these lie at the root of the assertion that the appearance stories in the gospels are not historical accounts of what took place.

APPEARANCES OF JESUS: ORIGINS OF THE EASTER TRADITION

The appearance stories in the gospels are "constructs" of the early Christian Tradition and the gospel writers. The realization of this leads to the question: What really happened? What is the origin of the stories of Jesus' appearances to various people? What sort of experience or experiences led to the development of a tradition that resulted in the appearance stories as we now have them in our gospels? There are two general approaches that various theologians have suggested.

The first approach, sometimes called the "inner psychological" approach, says that we can account for the emergence in Christian Tradition of stories of Jesus' appearances by grounding them in the faith convictions of his followers. In this approach, the claim is that some of Jesus' followers were so convinced that he was God's Chosen, God's Son, that God must have vindicated Jesus after he was put to death. This vindication took the form, these followers must have reasoned, of God raising Jesus to new life because that was the model for vindication that would have been part of their worldview. From this conviction, that God must have raised Jesus from the dead, came stories about the risen Jesus appearing to various people as the tradition about Jesus circulated among the early Christian communities. So, the dynamics of the emergence of the appearance stories went this way: faith convictions about Jesus led to the supposition that God had raised him from the dead, which led to stories of his appearances. The appearance stories, then, are ultimately grounded in faith, emerging from faith in Jesus.

Although this approach may be attractive to those who are suspicious of anything "supernatural" happening in our world, there are major difficulties with it. Perhaps the most important is that at Jesus' death, his followers do not seem to have displayed the great faith in him that such an approach would demand. All indications point to a state of confusion, disappointment, and even disillusionment in Jesus' followers. They did indeed eventually come to have faith in him, but how are we to account for this faith? It does not seem to have been there after the crucifixion in sufficient strength to ground the appearance tradition.

A second approach seems to be more satisfactory in explaining the emergence of the appearance tradition. This approach insists that the best way to account for the stories of Jesus' appearances to various people is to say that some of his followers were, in fact, seized by the presence of Jesus. Jesus, *alive*, entered into their consciousness "from outside" and unexpectedly. The gospel stories indicate surprise and amazement on the part of Jesus' followers. They were not looking for him to appear to them.

But what kind of experience did they have? Certain common features of the appearance stories may provide a clue. For one thing, they experienced the same Jesus they had experienced while he was with them before his death, yet he was also different. He now enters rooms without opening doors, for example, and he can simply disappear from their sight. There is a continuity (it *is* Jesus), but there is a discontinuity, too. This is no resuscitation of a corpse such that Jesus returns to his former earthly existence. Jesus was in touch with them from another dimension of existence.

The emphasis in the appearance tradition on seeing Jesus may provide us with another clue as to the nature of the appearances. As theologian Gerald O'Collins points out, although Paul uses a Greek word for seeing, *ophthe,* that can mean some kind of non-visionary revelation, the gospels use predominantly an active form of "to see" which emphasizes the activity of the witnesses. In other words, they *saw* Jesus, the gospel stories insist. It is plausible to say, then, that the appearance stories are based on visionary experiences of Jesus as alive, visions of Jesus that unexpectedly came upon his followers. And this changed their lives. They had a renewed and vigorous faith in him. They felt called to a profound conversion, to a different way of understanding and acting.[1]

EMPTY TOMB

The other question related to the resurrection tradition concerns the stories about certain women finding Jesus' tomb empty when they went there after his death. Do these stories have an historical basis to them or are they based on pure legend, arising from the supposition that since Jesus had risen, his tomb must have been empty?

For some theologians, the stories of finding the empty tomb are later additions to the appearance tradition and do not, then, have an historical basis. Not found in the earliest layer of the tradition about Jesus, they are "constructs," purely legendary in origin.[2] The earliest list of resurrection appearances in 1 Corinthians noted above, for example, makes no mention at all of finding an empty tomb. On the other hand, other theologians argue that the stories in the gospels about the empty tomb probably do have an historical basis because of the fact that all of them, although there are variations, are consistent in saying that women (or a woman in the case of John's gospel) find the tomb empty. This detail is considered important because in Jesus' time women were not regarded as qualified, reliable witnesses and so it is unlikely that a purely legendary story would emerge whose principal witnesses are women. Legend makers do not invent positively unhelpful material.[3]

THE THIRD DAY?

Added to the confusing historical scene, we have to take the chronology of the resurrection story into account, since we cannot take it for granted, even if the empty tomb stories have an historical basis, that the resurrection actually took place "on the third day" after the crucifixion of Jesus. Biblical scholars have noted that the phrase "on the third day" had become, in Jewish thinking, a way of talking about the arrival of the time of salvation and God's vindication of the elect. In Jewish apocalyptic literature, it was the term between the end of this world and the coming of the new. Thus, this expression may be a way of describing the belief that, with the experience of the risen Lord, the end time of salvation had come. The phrase came to be understood in a chronological way, but it is not at all certain that it was originally meant that way.[4]

The resurrection experience, as noted already, set off a missionary movement that resulted in the growth and development of the Christian church. In the tradition of this church, claims about who Jesus was and what he had done surfaced and came to be topics of intense discussion, even controversy. It is now time to go on to examine two of the most important claims: Jesus as Lord and Jesus as savior!

NOTES

1. See Gerald O'Collins, *Interpreting Jesus* (Mahwah, N.J.: Paulist Press 1976), pp. 116-119.

2. This is the position of Hans Küng, for example, in *On Being A Christian*, pp. 363-366.

3. These are the very words of Gerald O'Collins in *Interpreting Jesus* (Mahwah, N.J.: Paulist, 1976), p. 126.

4. See Bruce Vawter, *This Man Jesus* (Garden City, N.Y.: Doubleday; Image Books, 1975), pp. 42-46.

Questions for Reflection and Discussion

1. What comes to mind when you think of Jesus' resurrection? Have the suggestions of this chapter added to or changed your understanding? Explain.

2. Find the stories of Jesus' resurrection appearances in the New Testament. Make a list of the similarities and differences among them.

3. Look up the stories that recount the finding of the empty tomb in the New Testament. Make a list of the similarities and differences among them.

4. What is your reaction to the suggestion in this chapter that the followers of Jesus had visionary experiences of him? Is this suggestion a plausible one to you?

Suggested Readings

Brown, Raymond E. *The Virginal Conception and Bodily Resurrection of Jesus,* chapter 2. New York: Paulist, 1973.

Küng, Hans. *On Being A Christian,* pp. 343-410. Translated by Edward Quinn. Garden City, N.Y.: Doubleday, 1976.

O'Collins, Gerald. *Interpreting Jesus,* chapter 4. Mahwah, N.J.: Paulist, 1983.

Perkins, Pheme. *Resurrection: New Testament Witness and Contemporary Reflection.* Garden City, N.Y.: Doubleday, 1984.

CHAPTER FOURTEEN

JESUS AS LORD

You may have had the experience of hearing someone whisper "My Lord and my God" during the celebration of the Eucharist in your parish church as the priest raises the consecrated bread and wine. The raising of these elements follows the words the priest speaks, "This is my body...this is my blood," words Christian tradition attributes to Jesus at his final meal with his disciples, shortly before he was put to death. In Catholic tradition, the bread and wine at the Eucharist become Jesus' body and blood and Jesus is truly present. Thus, the response by many in the church, spoken in adoration: "My Lord and my God."

Many Christians would not say that Jesus is really present in the bread and wine, and would. But most, if not all, would agree that Jesus is God. He is no mere human being. And so he is the object of devotion and worship.

What does it mean to call Jesus God? Have you ever thought about it? Think about the last few chapters of this book. Have they made you feel uncomfortable with their emphasis on a very human Jesus? A student came into a teacher's office after class one day and apologized for having very hostile feelings toward her because of this. What she had been presenting in class was so contrary to what he had been taught and to his understanding of Jesus that he was very angry. And the reason for his anger was quite simple. The Christian Tradition he was raised in so stressed the divinity of Jesus that he thought of Jesus as divine, first and foremost, and not really human at all. The professor, too, had been brought up with this attitude. To talk of a very human Jesus was an affront to the student's sensitivities because it threatened his view of Jesus as divine.

Both of them, and many other Christians as well, were raised in a tradition that forgot the other aspect of Jesus that is likewise part of Christian Tradition, namely, that he was a real human being, not a god merely masquerading as one. This is precisely what contemporary theology tries to take seriously. But are we denying that Jesus is divine? In order to address this question, we can begin by outlining certain highlights in Christian Tradition's reflection on Jesus insofar as it concerns his divine and human dimensions.

JESUS AS DIVINE AND HUMAN

While it is impossible in this book to detail and discuss in depth the development of Christian thinking about the divine and human dimensions of Jesus, it is possible to identify a number of key moments and key concerns in this development. Of importance to note at the start is that it took a number of centuries for Christians to develop what they accepted as adequate categories of thought about Jesus. There was, in other words, a real development.

The New Testament itself witnesses to the fact that there was no unambiguous affirmation that Jesus was divine. The gospels of Matthew, Mark, and Luke show that there was a variety of ways of talking about Jesus: he was a teacher, a prophet, perhaps the prophet of the end times. Jesus was the Messiah, or the Son of God (the term in Jesus' day simply meant one of God's favored ones), or the Son of Man. None of these necessarily meant that Jesus was divine, but they all showed in some way a conviction that Jesus was related to God, even uniquely related to God: he was *the* Son of God. It is not really strange that there was no quick and easy identification of Jesus as God. The first Christians were Jews, and God was that ultimate reality that Jesus called his "Father." To posit an identity of Jesus with God would grossly offend the Jewish sense of monotheism. There was one God, alone. Their categories of thought and their religious sensitivities did not really allow them to make this move.

Yet it was made. John's gospel, written toward the end of the first century, carries the association of Jesus with God to the point of establishing a quasi-identity of Jesus with God. Jesus is, for the writer of John's gospel, the Word of God become flesh. This Word of God was with God from the beginning of time, is the creative principle of all things, and even *is* divine in some way. John does not confuse Jesus with God, the Father, but he does make of Jesus something more than simply another human being. There is something profoundly divine about Jesus. John thus writes in the prologue to his gospel (1:1–14):

> In the beginning was the Word, and the Word was with God, and the Word was God. He was in the beginning with God. All things came into being through him, and without him not one thing came into being. What has come into being in him was life, and the life was the light of all people. The light shines in the darkness, and the darkness did not overcome it.
>
> There was a man sent from God whose name was John. He came as a witness to testify to the light, so that all might believe through him. He himself was not the light, but he came to testify to the light. The true light, which enlightens everyone, was coming into the world
>
> He was in the world, and the world came into being through him; yet the world did not know him. He came to what was his own, and his own people did not accept him. But to all who received him who believed in his name, he gave power to become children of God, who were born, not of blood or of the will of the flesh or of the will of man, but of God.
>
> And the Word became flesh and lived among us, and we have seen his glory, the glory as of a father's only son, full of grace and truth.

This prologue is important because it came to reflect and influence the dominant way the Christian church articulated its understanding of who Jesus was in the centuries that followed.

Further articulation of who Jesus was occurred in the context of a number of controversies about Jesus. One of the first major controversies occurred toward the end of the first century and lasted into the third century. This was the controversy about what is called a *docetic* Christology. Groups of Christians were taking the divine aspect of Jesus so seriously that they refused to accept his humanity. There was among these groups a suspicion of, even a denigration of, the material world. God and the spiritual realm was alone good; anything related to material reality was evil. As divine, Jesus could not really be human and thus have a body and be associated with evil matter. He only *seemed* to be human, they said (hence, the term *docetism*, from the Greek *dokein*, "to seem"). Thus, there arose a movement to deny the real and complete humanity of Jesus.

This was rejected by leaders of the mainstream churches. There was a recognition that this approach failed to do justice to an aspect of Jesus felt to be an integral part of the received tradition about him, namely, his humanity. Whatever else one said about Jesus, however one understood his divinity, one could not deny that he was a real human being!

The Arian controversy of the fourth century dealt with another problem in the way Christians articulated their faith in Jesus. The issue in question centered on the relationship between the Word of God (or the Son) and the Father. A priest named Arius championed the view that the Word was a lesser kind of spiritual being than the Father. There could only be one God, Arius pointed out, and this was the Father. The Word might be called divine but did not really share the fullness of the divinity. A church council was held at Nicaea in present-day Turkey in 325 to deal with this matter; the council rejected the Arian position. In making the Word a lesser divinity, Arius was not doing justice to the belief that in Jesus—the Word become flesh—one really did encounter *God*, the one true God, and not some semi-divine reality.

Still another controversy arose not many years later, known as the *monophysite* controversy (from the Greek: *monos* means one and *physis* means nature). It centered on the relationship of the divine and the human in Jesus, such that both were preserved intact. This controversy came to a head when the teachings of a monk from Alexandria, Egypt, named Eutyches advocated the position that when the divine Logos (Word) took on flesh, the human nature of Jesus was so engulfed that it, in effect, ceased to exist. Jesus, therefore, had only one nature, a divine one. The effect was to deny the full and real humanity of Jesus.

The controversy that resulted from this view led to a church council at Chalcedon, also in present-day Turkey, and in 451 the Chalcedonian formula for understanding Jesus was set forth. This expression of faith insisted that the orthodox way of understanding Jesus had to include the ideas that in Jesus there was only one person (or *hypostasis*, a technical word that meant, roughly speaking, "one existing subject") whose very being was made up of two natures ("nature" meaning that which made something to be what is was, for example, a dog, a tree, or a human). These two natures came together in this one person in such a way that each retained its complete integrity. The Chalcedonian confession of faith reads:

> In agreement, therefore, with the holy fathers, we all unanimously teach that we should confess that our Lord Jesus Christ is one and the same Son, the same perfect in Godhead and the same perfect in [humanity], truly God and truly [human], the same of a rational soul and body, consubstantial with the Father in Godhead, and the same consubstantial with us in [humanity], like us in all things except sin; begotten from the Father before the ages as regards his Godhead, and in the last days, the same, because of us and because of our salvation begotten from the Virgin Mary, the [God-bearer], as regards his [humanity]; one and the same Christ, Son, Lord, only-begotten, made known in two natures without confusion, without change, without division, without separation, the difference of the natures being by no means removed because of the union, but the property of each nature being preserved and coalescing in one [person] and one [existing subject]—not parted or divided into two [persons] but one and the same Son, only-begotten, divine Word, the Lord Jesus Christ, as the prophets of old and Jesus Christ himself have taught us about him and the creed of our [ancestors] has handed down.[1]

The Council of Chalcedon, in fact, set the parameters for Christian reflection on Jesus from the fifth century to the present day. It did not explain *how* the two natures could be united in one person; it simply insisted that this was the case. Using the language of "person" and "nature" with the understandings of these words that were part of the cultural framework of fifth-century Christians, the Council expressed the faith of the Christian community in a way acceptable to the majority of that community and in a way that was viewed as capturing the truth of the tradition about Jesus.

A COPERNICAN REVOLUTION IN CHRISTOLOGY

As we have noted throughout this book, Christian teaching is always enunciated from a particular historical and cultural context, using the categories of thought provided by that context, and reflecting the particular emphases and concerns that Christians have in that time and place. In this regard, then, contemporary theologians are trying to formulate adequate ways of thinking about Jesus, ways that will be faithful to Christian Tradition and yet different because they reflect contemporary concerns, contemporary categories of thought, and contemporary sensitivities. Not to do this is to make Jesus irrelevant, a foreign "other" who is literally of another world and therefore unintelligible to us. It is time now to introduce the main directions in contemporary reflection on Jesus.

The Christology reflected in the Chalcedonian formula, above, that emerged from the Christological controversies of the fourth and fifth centuries is called the "classical" Christology. As we saw in Chapter Ten, it is a Christology "from above," a "descending" or "high" Christology. It is a way of understanding the reality of Jesus that begins by reflecting on Jesus as divine and then goes on to reflect on his humanity. At least it does this in theory. While this classical Christology did not intend this result, it in fact so emphasized the divinity of Jesus that it tended not to pay much attention to his humanity. Emphasis was on the *divine Word* who became human; everything else was sacrificed to this divine emphasis.

Contemporary Christology comes at the reality of Jesus from the opposite end. Such Christology begins reflection on Jesus by taking his humanity very seriously and by looking at the human, historical Jesus. In everyday language, it is a Christology "from below." When such reflection remains at the level of the human, historical Jesus, it is also called a "low" Christology. If it then proceeds to deal with the divine dimension of Jesus, it is a "low, ascending" Christology. The key thing to keep in mind is that the starting point for reflection on Jesus is the human Jesus. It takes his humanity very, very seriously: Jesus was a first-century Palestinian Jew and he reflected this in his thinking and acting.

Why this shift? In many ways, this shift is a result of the cultural situation in which Christian reflection—and indeed, the experience of Christians—occurs today. We do not live in a culture that takes it for granted that there is a God and that this God acted in and through Jesus. We live, rather, in a culture that is both religiously pluralistic and dominated by a secular mentality. We have our minds on things "below," as it were, that is, on the material realities and experiences of this world. The Transcendent, God, is not uppermost on our minds and is absent from our various institutions. Our consciousness does not deal easily or automatically with the divine and spiritual. Thus, beginning reflection on Jesus from the divine side, as the eternal divine Word, sounds strange to our ears and to those of our contemporaries. This approach does not resonate with our consciousness of, and our primary reactions to, reality. In this situation, then, it is more appropriate to begin with the human, historical person, Jesus of Nazareth.

UNDERSTANDING JESUS TODAY: JESUS AS SYMBOL OF GOD

The challenge facing Christians today is that of articulating an intelligible way of understanding Jesus and his relationship to God, taking his humanity and his human history seriously. In doing this, we must remain faithful to the underlying conviction of Christian Tradition that received a classical expression at Chalcedon, namely, that when it comes to understanding Jesus of Nazareth, one must insist that the reality of God and the reality of humankind are united in Jesus. We have to come up with categories of thought that do this. One such category is that of "symbol."

To begin with, then, what is a symbol? Chapter Seven, on religious language, touched somewhat on this. A symbol is a thing, event, or person that puts us in touch with something else. Our gaze and our understanding does not stop at a symbol, but rather "passes through" the symbol to that "something else." We are brought into contact with this something else in and through the symbol.

A symbol is more than a sign, although the two are often used interchangeably. A sign points to something else, makes us aware of something else, to be sure, but in a way that can be called extrinsic and arbitrary to that something else. Take a stop sign, for example. It is in the shape of an octagon and it is red. When we see it, we become aware of the fact that we must stop. But the shape and the color are simply conventional and perhaps practical. Red stands out, at least in daylight, and so is noticeable. Hence, it was considered to be a good color for a stop sign. But why not some other color, one that might be even more noticeable? And why the octagon? Could not another shape, say, a square, do? There is no intrinsic necessity for stop signs that are red octagons. We might all decide that it is better to have square stop signs painted some outlandish, but more noticeable, color, and there doesn't seem to be anything wrong with that except for the practical problem and expense of changing all the signs.

Symbols are different. There is a much deeper connection between the symbol and what it symbolizes than between a sign and what it points to. There is some intrinsic, inherent, essential connection. If one takes the color red as an example, this color often appears as a symbol of violence and bloodshed. When properly used, it evokes an awareness of, even a sense of, violence. An author or artist could not simply and arbitrarily replace red with another color, say, white or turquoise and still retain the same impact and sense of what the color red symbolizes.

The symbol and what it symbolizes come together in a profound way, then, such that a deep unity exists between them. There is a joining of the two realities, a connectedness that goes beyond the merely conventional and arbitrary, and allows the reality of what is symbolized to appear in and through the symbol. The symbol can be said to *participate* in the reality of what it symbolizes, and this makes their connectedness profound. To put this another way, the symbol can be said to be another mode of existing on the part of what is symbolized.

An analogy will help to explain and to reinforce this idea. We humans are appropriately thought of as *embodied subjects*. As subjects, we have a degree of self-determination and we are centers of consciousness. There is an autonomous "I" that is the center for our experiencing the world and it is free in a limited way. This dimension of the human person is a person's spiritual nature. Yet this subjective, spiritual aspect of the human person is enfleshed, or incarnated. We are not pure subjects or pure spirits. We have bodies. We exercise our self-determination (our freedom) and we express who we are in and through our bodies. Our physical selves become the media in and through which our spiritual, interior selves are revealed. Who we are and the exercise of our autonomy are expressed in and through the actions of, and the relationships created by, our physical selves. These outer, physical aspects of us as we relate to the outer, physical aspects of everything around us really express who we are as free, self-determining subjects. This way of understanding the human person, as enfleshed spirit, can be used as an analogy to what goes on in symbolic mediation. The symbol is an expression of what is symbolized, as our physical actions are expressions of our interior, spiritual selves.

Although there is an inherent identity between the symbol and the reality mediated through the symbol, there is also a distinction. The reality to which the symbol points is other than the symbol itself. We do not stop at the symbol, but rather "go through it" to come into contact with that "other" that the symbol brings into consciousness. The symbol is what is symbolized, in that it really puts us in touch with that reality; yet it is not what is symbolized because it is, at the same time, something other. We have to look through the symbol to the symbolized reality. There is a unity or an identity of sorts, yet there is also a difference. One must not confuse the two.

When it comes to understanding a *religious* symbol, we can say that a religious symbol is any thing, event, or person that puts us in touch with the reality of the Divine. One could say that it is a medium through which we encounter the transcendent Other we call God. To put it another way, a religious symbol is the medium through which the transcendent mystery that is God comes into contact with us.

JESUS OF NAZARETH AS THE SYMBOL OF GOD

If we apply the category of religious symbol to Jesus of Nazareth, we can say that Jesus is the symbol of God, and as such, makes God present to us in and through his humanity and his human history. But Christians make further claims about Jesus. Jesus is not only a symbol of God, a medium in and through whom the reality of God is experienced, but he is the definitive and normative medium of God. There may be other symbols, other media, in and through which humans encounter the Divine; but Jesus is, for Christians, the ultimate symbol.

How are the reality of God and the reality of humankind united in this understanding of Jesus? They are united in the sense that the symbol and what it symbolizes are united. As explained above, the symbol makes present or mediates the reality (or aspects of the reality) of what is symbolized. Because of this, there is a real sense in which the symbol is a form of expression of what is symbolized. The whole argument that Jesus is the symbol of God and thereby unites in his person divinity and humanity rests on this crucial affirmation about the power and nature of symbols. We can thus say that Jesus, as the ultimate symbol of the Divine, is the model expression of the Divine and really makes the Divine present. In this way Jesus of Nazareth, in all his actions and attitudes, in his very person, is truly God and truly human.

Of course, no finite medium or symbol can ever capture or mediate the complete reality of the Divine. This is the case with Jesus, too. Jesus of Nazareth, a finite human being, cannot possibly capture everything about the God who is experienced in and through his life and person. The Divine is not exhausted in Jesus; there is more to God than even Jesus can mediate. Yet Christians believe that Jesus brings us into contact with the Divine in a definitive way that is normative. To say that Jesus does not reveal the complete reality of God is not to denigrate the importance and centrality of who he is. It is, rather, to recognize the truth about the reality of symbols, especially symbols of God.

Maleness of Jesus

This insistence that the symbol is not univocally what it symbolizes is important to remember in light of our recognition of the equal dignity of women and men. The Christian tradition has used the fact of Jesus' maleness as an indication of the inherent superiority of the male to the female. God chose to be present in and through a man, not a woman, because of the superiority of men, the argument went. A woman, lesser in status, could not adequately reveal God. In reaction to this, many women today find a male symbol of God untenable, saying it reinforces those outmoded and damaging views.

But is *maleness* inherent in the symbol of God? Jesus was a male. Was it necessary for God to be revealed in and through a male? One line of thought says "yes and no" to this. No, if by necessity one means that because of their superior nature men alone can truly symbolize the Divine. Yes, if by necessity one means that because of the cultural context in which God revealed the Divine Self, such revelation would not be received through a woman. The argument is that the historical, cultural context in which God in fact revealed the Divine Self was a patriarchal one in which women were excluded from positions of leadership, and especially religious leadership. They were not counted as credible witnesses in legal cases. Who would really listen to a woman preaching the same message Jesus preached? Would a woman in Jesus' day even have thought it possible to do so?

We can say, then, that it is not the maleness of Jesus that is crucial to his being a symbol of the Divine. Rather, it is the values he had, the attitudes he displayed, the dispositions he held, and the sensitivities that dominated his life that more adequately bring us in touch with the Divine. And these are not gender specific.

In this chapter, we have focused on a way of understanding Jesus as Lord, as the unique and *ultimate symbol of the Divine*, in order to develop an understanding of him that preserves his utter and complete humanity and takes his human history seriously. Both of these are essential in any Christology that is to make sense today. Yet this is not all there is to Jesus. Christian Tradition has insisted that God comes into contact with us not simply to give us information about the Divine Self, but to *save and heal* us. It is this fundamental dimension of the Christian faith that we must now consider.

NOTE

1. Taken from JND Kelly, *Early Christian Doctrines.* Revised edition (San Francisco: Harper & Row, 1978), pp. 339-340. I have made Kelly's translation more inclusive in its language, substituting "humanity" for "man."

QUESTIONS FOR REFLECTION AND DISCUSSION

1. Think about the understanding of Jesus you had before reading this chapter. Are the suggestions of this chapter different? Similar? Elaborate.

2. What is your reaction to the "low" Christology of this chapter?

3. What is your reaction to the use of the category "symbol" to understand how divinity and humanity come together in Jesus?

4. Do you think that as a real human being Jesus can elicit from you an attitude of allegiance and devotion?

SUGGESTED READINGS

Hill, Brennan. *Jesus, the Christ: Contemporary Perspectives,* chapter 10. Mystic, Conn.: Twenty-Third Publications, 1991.

Johnson, Elizabeth A. *She Who Is: The Mystery of God in Feminist Theological Discourse,* chapters 7, 8, and 9. New York: Crossroad, 1992.

O'Collins, Gerald. *Interpreting Jesus,* chapters 6 and 7. Mahwah, N.J.: Paulist Press, 1983.

Sloyan, Gerard S. *Jesus: Redeemer and Divine Word.* Wilmington, Del.: Michael Glazier, 1989.

CHAPTER FIFTEEN

JESUS AS SAVIOR

In its story of the early Christian church, the Acts of the Apostles (4:11–12) presents a speech by Peter to a number of Jewish rulers, elders, and doctors of the law in Jerusalem. He proclaims:

This Jesus is
"the stone that was rejected by you, the builders;
it has become the cornerstone."
There is salvation in no one else, for there is no other name under heaven given among mortals by which we must be saved.

The Nicene Creed, with its classical Christology, says about the coming of Christ: "For our sake and *for our salvation*, he came down from heaven." Both of these capture the Christian conviction that Jesus is not simply divine; he is our *savior*.

What does this mean? From what are we saved? And what role does Jesus play in our salvation? Earlier in this book, you were asked to reflect on your experience of life and identify what you felt was wrong with the world and with your life. All of us, in various ways, experience something amiss in life, and we yearn for and seek a remedy for our plighted situation. This is at the root of what Christians call the search for salvation.

The connection between Jesus and salvation emerges from the message and activity of the historical Jesus. The kingdom of God is on its way! God is coming, and things are going to be all right! Anything that diminishes or harms our existence will be done away with! Change your ways and believe in this good news! That was, in effect, the central message of Jesus. And Jesus did more than announce the coming of God's kingdom. Through his healings and exorcisms he was playing an active part in its establishment.

For many Jews of Jesus' time, as noted in Chapter Eleven, this would have meant the restoration of Israel freed from Roman rule, a restoration that would result in a condition of peace, justice, and prosperity. This might involve doing away with the present and the setting up of an entirely new order: a new heaven and a new earth (the apocalyptic view). For Jesus, it involved being at one with God, acknowledging God as our true god. It involved being healed from physical ailments and from the control of devils (the miracles of Jesus). It involved a change in attitudes and actions that resulted in healing from whatever oppressed and diminished human existence.

The early Christians developed the link between Jesus and salvation that was present in his ministry, and the New Testament reflects the direction their understanding took. They came to understand Jesus as savior in that he atoned for human sinfulness by his death on the cross. There was a real sense that the key to salvation lay in the reconciliation between God and human beings. The root cause of the human predicament was that humans had turned away from God.

The idea of the atoning death of a just person or persons bringing about reconciliation between God and humans was an idea "in the air" in Jesus' culture. It is evident in the books of the Maccabees concerning the Jewish martyrs who were killed in the uprising against the Syrian oppression under the reign of Antiochus IV in the second century B.C.E. The martyrdom of one just person atoned for the sins of the nation (see 2 Maccabees 7:37f. This notion is also present in a poem in Isaiah (52:13–53:12) about the servant of Yahweh, dating from the sixth century B.C.E. This servant, who many scholars think represents the nation of Israel and its sufferings, is persecuted and made to suffer. This atones for everyone's sins, thereby bringing health and healing to all.

The suffering servant figure seems to have shaped the early Christian consciousness and provided the first communities with a way of understanding the death of Jesus.[1] We thus see in the letters of Paul the idea that Jesus' death on the cross was "for us," a death by which Jesus, as our representative, atoned for human sin.[2] We read in the gospels references to Jesus talking about his death as a death "for many," reflecting this same notion of vicarious atonement.[3] In a different way, but capturing the same thought, the letter to the Hebrews describes Jesus' death as a sacrifice, replacing the sacrifice of bulls on the Jewish feast of the Atonement. On this great feast, a bull was sacrificed in the Temple, a ritual that was considered an act of atonement by which the sins of the people were forgiven. Jesus' sacrifice on the cross replaces this yearly ritual, according to the author of this letter. It is a once-and-for-all act that atones for human sin definitively.

The New Testament theme of atonement, according to which the death of Jesus is the primary act that brings about reconciliation between God and humankind, influenced the development of Christian reflection on the saving work of Jesus, as Christians tried to articulate their understanding of how he was our savior. Over the course of many years of reflection, three prominent ways of understanding this emerged: Jesus breaking the devil's hold on humankind; Jesus paying satisfaction to God to make up for human sin; and Jesus suffering in our place the punishment due to human sinfulness. Let us examine each of these.

Ransoming Humanity from the Devil's Grip

During the seventh to eleventh centuries, one of the dominant ways of understanding Jesus' saving work involved the idea of Christ overcoming the right of the devil to have dominion over humankind. Pope Gregory the Great, at the end of the sixth century, was one of a number of thinkers to articulate this. He lived at a time of widespread belief in the presence and activity of all manner of supernatural forces, both good and evil. Gregory reflected an understanding of the human situation which held that humankind, because of the sin of Adam (note the patriarchal culture which neglects Eve: the man represents all humanity), was thereby under the power of the devil. This state of bondage was a just one because Adam had freely sinned, and thus the devil had "rights" over him and his descendants, who inherited this situation. Adam had turned away from God to the devil. Thus, all human beings were born into a state of captivity, and, as sinners, were subject to death and damnation in the realm of the devil after death, banished from the enjoyment of God's presence. The important point in this theory was that the devil had the right to exercise dominion over human beings.[4]

Gregory argued that God did not leave humans in such a plight. The situation could be reversed, he and many others of his time thought, if the devil did what he had no right to do and thus lose his dominion over human beings. To this end, God became human in Jesus, a sinless person. That Jesus was divine was not, however, apparent to the devil, who tried to exercise dominion over Jesus. The devil throws himself against him (for example, the temptations in the desert) and drags him down into death, one of his rights over sinners. But Jesus was not a sinner. The devil was overstepping his bounds, trying to take possession of what he had no right to. This resulted, to Gregory, in the devil losing his right to hold power over humankind, because Jesus, like Adam, represented all humanity. Moreover, since Jesus was divine, the devil could not hold him among the dead in hell. Jesus rises triumphantly from the grip of the devil and ascends to God's realm. The power of the devil was thus overcome.

SATISFYING FOR SIN

From the twelfth century even up to the present time, a prominent way of understanding Christ's saving work centers on the idea of Christ paying the "satisfaction" due to God because of humankind's sin in Adam. This satisfaction model was elaborated in a highly systematic way in the twelfth century by Anselm, bishop of Canterbury, England. Reflecting his medieval feudal context, Anselm looked back on the sin of Adam and saw it as a sin that offended the honor and dignity of God. Adam had disobeyed his Lord, God, and in Anselm's day this was to offend and challenge the essential order of reality itself: vassals owed their lords obedience. In order to set things right, the offense had to be atoned for. In the legal system of Anselm's culture, this involved reparation and something extra to make up for the offense in some way: satisfaction.

In the case of Adam's sin, there was a further complicating factor. The nature of the crime depended on the status of the one offended. More satisfaction had to be paid to a king than to a merchant, for example. Since God was the offended party, this meant that the reparation and satisfaction had to be commensurate with the infinite dignity and status of God. This, however, made the situation impossible. Since humans sinned (in Adam), they had to make up for the offense. But sinful, finite humans could not. A human being could do nothing that had an infinite status to it which alone could repair the damage done. What is more, Anselm argued that God could not simply forgive the offense. That would be to treat sinner and righteous alike, which would be inconsistent with the principle of justice. The situation seemed hopeless. Here is where God's mercy entered the scene, according to Anselm. A mere human being may not be able to atone for the sin of Adam, but someone who is both God and human could. And so God became human, in order to set things right and pay the satisfaction.

Jesus set things right again, first of all, by being our representative and being completely obedient to God, the Father, thereby reversing Adam's disobedience. And his freely offered death was the act of satisfaction. He was obedient to God, which was what he owed God in virtue of his human status; but as a sinless person, he did not have to suffer death, one of the effects of Adam's sin. Yet Jesus freely allowed himself to be put to death, offering this to God as the satisfaction, the "something extra," to make up for Adam's sin. Because of his infinite dignity as divine, Jesus' act of satisfaction fulfilled the demands of justice. Indeed, so meritorious was it that it could be applied to all humans. Thus the great sin of Adam was overcome and humans could once again be at one with God.

Penal Substitution

The third way of understanding the saving work of Christ involves the notion of penal substitution. Although not unique to John Calvin, it emerges in a classic way in his writings in the sixteenth century and is held among a number of evangelicals today. In this view, the sin of our first parents deserved God's wrath. This wrath was borne for us by Jesus. God the Father vents the divine wrath on Jesus, and this wrath is thereby appeased. Jesus' passion and death are thus the penalty he pays, for us, to appease God's righteous anger. As a result, humans can be at one with God again. Calvin wrote in his *Institutes of the Christian Religion:*

> It is especially worthwhile to ponder the analogy set forth by Paul: "Christ . . . became a curse for us," etc. [Galatians 3:13]. It was superfluous, even absurd, for Christ to be burdened with a curse, unless it was to acquire righteousness for others by paying what they owed. Isaiah's testimony [53:5] is also clear: "The chastisement of our peace was laid upon Christ, and with his stripes healing has come upon us." For unless Christ had made satisfaction for our sins, it would not have been said that he appeased

God by taking upon himself the penalty to which we were subject. The words that follow in the same passage agree with this: "I have stricken him for the transgression of my people" [Isaiah 53:8]. Let us add the interpretation of Peter, which will remove all uncertainty: "He . . . bore our sins . . . on the tree" [1 Peter 2:24]. He is saying that the burden of condemnation, from which we were freed, was laid upon Christ.[5]

A Renewed Understanding of Jesus' Saving Work

These three ways of understanding the saving work of Jesus reflect the cultural milieu in which those who articulated them lived. This has been a consistent theme in this book. All of our beliefs, our scriptures, our theology, come from us as we react to and make sense of the reality of God impinging upon our existence. So, the scriptural witness reflects the notion of sacrifice as a way of atoning for human sinfulness, an idea that was part of the Jewish religious consciousness of Jesus' day. Gregory the Great reflected his culture's preoccupation with supernatural forces and notions of rights, even the rights of the devil. Anselm reflects his feudal milieu, with its social order and legal system. The penal substitution theory reflects an unnuanced reading of biblical texts, taken as divinely revealed statements of fact. It regards statements from Isaiah 53 in this way, which talks about the suffering servant of God taking on the sins of many in the pain he bears and of being punished for them.

These models, however, reflect cultural perspectives we, in our culture, do not necessarily share. Why, for example, should God demand the death of a sacrificial victim for forgiveness to occur? Why should God want to vent anger on Christ to appease the divine anger? If one thinks of the parable of the prodigal son in Luke (15:11–32), the father, the figure of God in the parable, accepts the wayward son back freely and with rejoicing. There is no anger, no demand for punishment. What is more, the traditional models outlined above far from reflect the historical situation and events of Jesus' life. The task of Christians today is to continue the work attempted by these traditional models and articulate how Jesus saves us from what harms and diminishes human existence today. What follows is an outline of a way that holds promise for understanding this essential Christian teaching of salvation.

Jesus as Savior: A Contemporary Approach

In the analysis of Original Sin in Chapter Nine, we saw that the root cause of our sinful state, and our root sin, is our attempt to be God or to replace God by idols, whether material things, pleasures, other persons, nations, or ourselves. The attempt to dominate others that results from this, and the consequent struggles and hurts caused by this, or our enslavement to what we think will satisfy us, leads to harm and diminishment in many ways. In this context, Jesus comes as our savior. But how does he save us? How does he free us from the situations and attitudes that cause harm?

An important thing to note at the start is that the salvation under discussion here is more than simply "getting to heaven" or "saving our souls." It includes what the Old Testament tradition called *shalom*, that is, total peace, justice, and healing. And it includes this *shalom* in the here and now. The traditional ideas about salvation missed this as they tended to emphasize our reconciliation with God and the resulting ability to escape from this "vale of tears" into a better world on the other side of death. While salvation does include this other world, contemporary Christian thought also looks to this world and sees salvation as affecting it. Salvation involves the transformation of the present situation in which we live. It certainly involved this for the historical Jesus. For example, God's healing power was real and effective, through Jesus, in his world as he effected amazing cures and exorcisms. But the question remains: What does Jesus do in bringing us toward salvation now, in our time?

An intelligible and useful approach is to see Jesus as introducing into our consciousness a way of being human and living that, when made real in our personal and corporate lives, results in our being freed from the attitudes and situations that cause us diminishment and harm. To put this positively, Jesus' attitudes and values can lead to building a world that promotes the well-being of humans and all creation. Jesus embodies a "new humanity," showing us how to truly live as "saved" persons in a saved world.

We can understand this if we focus on the various master-slave relationships humans have created. They are at the very root of much of the human predicament. We humans have set up relationships where we "look after number one," whether ourselves, our society, or our group. Centering on ourselves, we have alienated others or attempted to subordinate them. We have set up a world of insiders and outsiders, those who dominate and those who are dominated—"us" and "them."

Jesus, though, embodied and lived a different possibility of human living. By so doing, he shows us a way out of the predicament we have created for ourselves.

In his life, for example, he manifested a deep concern for the marginalized of his society. God's *shalom*—God's healing, saving power—was offered to "them," even if they were despised and regarded with contempt. This reaching out to the unloved and unwanted is an aspect of Jesus' life that we are challenged to make our own. Who are the marginalized in our society? How can we work for their inclusion and healing? These are questions we can ask and strive to answer as we attempt to make the attitudes and values of Jesus our own.

In his deeds and teachings, Jesus was critical of people who lorded it over others and were concerned with getting and maintaining power over others. He saw his life as one of service to others. Mark 10:45 expresses this attitude, an attitude that stuck in the memory of the early Christian Tradition: "The Son of Man came not to be served but to serve. . . ." He strongly criticized his disciples when they attempted to dominate each other, seeking to be "number one." Mark's gospel recalls Jesus' teaching.

> You know that among the Gentiles those whom they recognize as their rulers lord it over them. But it is not so among you; but whoever wishes to become great among you must be your servant, and whoever wishes to be first among you must be the slave of all.

Service to others for their welfare is a pervading frame of mind in the life of Jesus. To the extent we make this attitude real in our lives and in the social environment we create, we advance the establishment of a world of *shalom*, a healed or at least healing world. This way of living is implicitly critical of the widespread drive today in our individual and corporate lives to desire more for ourselves, to be the master, and to be concerned only for *our* well-being.

Jesus' attitude toward the God he called "Father" is also an important element in the establishment of a healed world. The gospels indicate that Jesus lived with a strong sense of being accepted by God, loved by God. He did not have to strive to justify himself or his work, or to be judged worthy in the eyes of others. This freed him from excessive self-concern, enabling him to be open to others and their concerns. Embracing the mind set of Jesus can be a powerfully liberating factor in our lives, as well. The God Jesus called *abba*, dear Father, is *abba* for us, too. We count. We are accepted and loved and, like the Prodigal son, we are forgiven. The realization of this frees us to be concerned for others.

We are led to the realization, by Jesus' life, that there is another direction our lives can take. Indeed, Jesus challenges us to follow him. This is the way that leads to a world redeemed and healed, in which the destructive tendencies and forces that diminish human well-being are overcome.

Some dimensions of this way of understanding Jesus as savior need further reflection. Salvation, seen in this light, is a process. We are not "saved" by Jesus as if salvation were simply given to us and everything were made right. The non-healing, sinful values and attitudes that are part of our very beings, the non-healing social institutions that we create, all of these are not automatically done away with just because Jesus introduces into our consciousness a new alternative for living. We are called to make Jesus' possibility for living real in our lives and in our institutions.

The structures and institutions we have created are included in the process of salvation. No social institution—our media, educational system, political system, or economic system—is value neutral. All promote and perpetuate ways of understanding who we are and what really counts in life. All cause some form of harm or distortion to our true selves as Jesus has revealed what a "true self" is. This is because social structures are set up by humans and reflect the sinfulness that profoundly affects human existence. Salvation, then, is not simply a personal and private thing. Humans, indeed, need to heal their personal lives, but they must also look at the harmful effects of the institutions they create or tolerate.

Just as the kingdom of God, for Jesus, was already present but not yet fully realized, there is a present-but-not-yet dimension to salvation. The "new humanity" modeled by Jesus and the efforts of his followers to make his vision of reality concrete have made salvation present here and now. But our experience teaches us that we will probably never fully realize salvation on this side of the grave: its completion remains in the future. The traditional doctrine of Original Sin with its teaching that we are slaves to sin reflects this truth about our situation. And so, the Christian hope in a heaven, or Jesus' image of the kingdom of God fully realized where all will be well and total salvation pertains, is an important element in the understanding of salvation. Salvation is a process that begins in the here and now, but it involves and is completed in a state of being that exists in the future, after death. Human existence is a pilgrimage toward a final goal that is realized partially, in degrees, by what we do now. This trust in a fulfilled future is important because it provides hope for the journey and its inevitable disappointments. Our strivings and our yearnings are not in vain.

This process of salvation that begins here, in this world, and which affects the way we build our world, is a process that we undertake not on our own, but with God's help. This is the faith experience of the Christian tradition, a faith experience that is captured, for example, in the Acts of the Apostles, where God's Spirit is the driving force behind the spread of the church. God, Christians insist, does not leave us on our own. God is an ever-present reality enabling us to make salvation real. But God does not force us to do this. We respond to God, or we fail to. And so, the Christian tradition has the notion of hell. It reminds us that salvation is not automatic, a process that is successful despite ourselves. God may help us and be present to us, but we have responsibility in the process.

JESUS' DEATH AND RESURRECTION

The death and resurrection of Jesus merit special attention. First of all, with respect to the death of Jesus, the Christian tradition has seen this as the act *par excellence* to bring about our salvation. The traditional ways of understanding this, present in the models outlined earlier in this chapter, sound strange to us today. A more adequate way of understanding the meaning of Jesus' death will be one that is faithful to the historical circumstances surrounding the event. His death cannot be separated from his life. As we have seen, Jesus' death, in historical terms, was brought about by what he said and did, particularly by his radical criticism of the existing social and religious institutions and customs.

What is the importance of the death of Jesus, as we try to grasp his role as savior? The saving work of Jesus is best seen, in the approach outlined above, in his whole life and person, not just in his death. This is what makes the "new humanity" real for us, the alternative way of living that Jesus proposed and exemplified that is the essence of salvation. His death might be considered as the supreme manifestation of what he stood for, summing up his entire life. Confronted with the hostility of those who were threatened by his vision of reality, Jesus did not abandon his views in order to save himself. This "man for others" was so much the servant of others, so concerned for their well-being, that he was willing to sacrifice himself for this vision. This way of understanding Jesus' death is even more reinforced if Jesus indeed understood it as an atonement or as part of the eschatological woes that preceded the end time and the coming of salvation.

The death of Jesus is also a powerful reminder both of the cost of following his way of life and of the extensive suffering that the non-healing ways of living we create can cause. In a very real way, Jesus represents all those who struggle for a more human way of living, in which all are nurtured and the welfare of all is of primary concern. Those who enjoy their special status and those who are afraid of venturing into the unknown, away from certainty and "security" (even though it may be harmful and destructive), do not change their ways easily. They strike out at the "odd" and subversive ways of those who point to a better order of things. The salvation that Jesus embodies and initiates is a salvation that does not come without struggle and pain.

The struggle and pain of the process of salvation would be all but unbearable, and the lack of success that we experience would make the process seemingly a hopeless one—but for the resurrection. To his earliest followers, the experience of Jesus as alive with God was an experience that vindicated him and what he stood for. God was truly on his side; God truly showed Jesus favor and approval. The resurrection can mean the same for us. Jesus' cause is God's cause and there is real hope in its ultimate realization. The future is not completely up to us, under our control; the future is in God's hands, too. The experience of Jesus raised to new life grounds our hope that new life is possible and, even more, that it will have the final word. The resurrection, then, is an empowering event, freeing us from the despair of hopelessness.

The "saving event" is, we can say, the whole life, death, and resurrection of Jesus of Nazareth. It not only opens us up to a new possibility for living, one that will free us from the distortions of our existence, but it is also an empowering event. Humans are given hope that the new humanity embodied in Jesus is an attainable reality, that it is worth beginning the process of realization in their individual and corporate lives.

Notes

1. See, for example, the discussion in Gerald O'Collins, *Interpreting Jesus* (Mahwah, N.J.: 1983), pp. 90-92.

2. See 1 Thessalonians 5:10; 1 Corinthians 15:3; Romans 4:25; 8:32.

3. See Mark 10:45, 14:22–24; Matthew 26:26–29.

4. See the discussion of this in Jeffery Hopper, *Understanding Modern Theology II: Reinterpreting Christian Faith for Changing Worlds* (Philadelphia: Fortress, 1987), pp. 14-17.

5. John Calvin, *The Institutes of the Christian Religion,* volume II, edited by John T. McNeill, translated and indexed by Ford Lewis Battles (Philadelphia: Westminster, 1960), p. 532.

QUESTIONS FOR REFLECTION AND DISCUSSION

1. How had you thought of Jesus as savior before you read this chapter? Did your understanding make sense to you? Explain.

2. Have you ever heard a description of Jesus as savior that reflects any of the three traditional models this chapter presents? Elaborate if you have, and give your reaction.

3. How would you summarize the way this chapter explains how Jesus is savior? What is your reaction to this?

4. Name some of the "distortions" of your existence. Could the values and attitudes of Jesus help in the overcoming of these? Explain.

SUGGESTED READINGS

Hill, Brennan R. *Jesus the Christ: Contemporary Perspectives.* Mystic, Conn.: Twenty-Third Publications, 1991. See especially chapters 11, 12.

O'Collins, Gerald. *Interpreting Jesus.* Mahwah, N.J.: Paulist Press, 1983. See especially chapter 5.

Ruether, Rosemary Radford. *To Change the World: Christology and Cultural Criticism.* New York: Crossroad, 1981.

Thompson, William M. *The Jesus Debate: A Survey and Synthesis.* Mahwah, N.J.: Paulist Press, 1985. See especially chapters 8–15.

CONCLUSION

Throughout the course of this book, there has been reference to a Copernican revolution taking place in Christian thinking today, with major ramifications for the way Christians understand themselves and, indeed, for the way they look at all of reality. By way of conclusion, the central aspect of this needs to be emphasized.

The most important and far-reaching feature of the revolution in Christian thinking today is the recognition of the profoundly human dimension to Christian Tradition. While not denying the activity and presence of the Divine, and insisting that the Divine makes its presence felt and that this stands at the base of Christianity, the active involvement of human beings in the development of Christianity is now being acknowledged seriously. People are not merely passive receptors of God's activity toward them. They condition and shape the experience such that there is a real interaction between the Divine and the human. This understanding was largely ignored in past generations of Christian reflection when the emphasis was very heavily on the divine side of things, to the neglect of the human.

The human involvement in shaping and articulating the experience of the Divine means that all the institutional expressions that make concrete the Christian response to God will be historically and culturally limited and conditioned. Scripture itself, the church's creeds, the institutional structures of the church—all have been culturally conditioned reactions to God as particular humans living in particular times and places with their particular worldviews have experienced God.

This has led to one of the most crucial problems facing Christian communities today: how do we discern and pass on the permanently valid "truth" that is expressed in and through these culturally conditioned and particular expressions? Indeed, is there a permanently valid truth for all times that will never need rethinking and new articulation? How does one recognize it, if it exists?

There is such a thing as truth that transcends its culturally conditioned expressions, although it always appears in and through these. This is the case in those human expressions of truth that become "classics," whether secular or religious. Certain writings seem to have the capacity for "grabbing us" with their truth. When we read or hear them, we recognize that they convey valid insights, valid "truths," about reality. There is a certain self-authentication that allows them to stand forth as expressions of the truth about reality which we intuitively sense.

When it comes to Christian Tradition, the most basic expression of permanently valid truth is the person and life of Jesus of Nazareth. Scripture and the teachings of the church are "true" to the extent that they mediate this person and, in particular, his values. Jesus is the model of what it means to be truly human, the model of "saved" humanity. He makes real the values and attitudes that are permanently valid for all times and places; this leads to authentic human existence in all of its dimensions—personal and social. In this sense he truly is "the way, the truth, and the life." But he is our model in a particular and culturally conditioned way. Christians are called not to imitate him slavishly and to consider his words literally as statements of unconditioned truth. Rather, they are called to make real in their lives and to articulate truths that make real in their particular circumstances the values and attitudes that are imaged in his life.

We are not, because of this, condemned to a groundless relativism where everything is valid and nothing is permanent. Yet the acceptance of Jesus as the concrete expression of permanently valid truth requires an act of faith. We may be grabbed by this "truth," but we must make an act of faith that it is indeed the truth. Furthermore, it must be verified by the living of it. No amount of rational argumentation will suffice.

To repeat a sentiment at the beginning of this volume: this book is intended to be an introduction to the exciting field of Christian theology. If it serves the purpose of putting the reader onto a new and enlivening pathway of reflection, it will have served its purpose. Great changes are taking place in Christian thinking in our day. I hope the reader will feel drawn into the theological enterprise so that the search for the truth and the commitment to it will continue and, indeed, become more and more part of the reader's life.

INDEX